TESTIMONIALS

George Tinsley, Sr. is widely respected as a successful entrepreneur, astute businessman, devoted community leader, and extraordinary visionary. To be sure, these descriptors reflect the man and his accomplishments. His achievements in business and in leadership cannot be overstated. In delivering above-target results, he is a force of nature. What makes George unique is his ability to make the inconceivable conceivable and the impossible possible. His personal relentlessness is fueled by an undiluted purpose and passion that is grounded in his values and his faith. This capability coupled with his deep generosity of spirit make him formidable in the face of life's challenges in whatever form they appear. From poverty and racism to any existing socioeconomic barrier, George triumphs. Because of this ability, "obstacles" are always "opportunities" to him. He is nothing short of a force of nature in his belief in the human spirit. His life is a testament to that belief. His story teaches us the importance of that belief. Inspiring doesn't begin to describe his journey.

—**Roseanna DeMaria**

roseanna@demariagroup.com

http://demariagroup.com/

http://www.linkedin.com/in/roseannademaria

Catch as Catch Can is an inspiring life story. Dr. T shares his life story, growing up, overcoming many obstacles. I have known him for over twenty-five years as a friend, business partner, and an inspiring mentor. Thank you, George, for sharing your journey—you have given so much to many.

—Derryl O. Benton
Chief Development Officer

HMSHost, Hudson, Dufry by Avolta

George Tinsley, Sr. is an entrepreneurial genius who has demonstrated an exceptional ability to turn his visions into reality. His unwavering dedication to community service and uplifting others is truly commendable. George is not only a remarkable athlete and entrepreneur but also the embodiment of perseverance. Despite facing challenges along his journey, he has consistently demonstrated resilience and determination.

—Karyn D. Bullock
Choo Smith Youth Empowerment, Inc.

Chief of Business and Economic Affairs

George Tinsley is a true American rags-to-riches story. He was impoverished as a boy growing up in Louisville with his grandmother. He came to Kentucky Wesleyan College on an academic and basketball scholarship in 1965 with everything he owned in a single grocery bag. Tinsley took advantage of the opportunities during his college career. He earned the highest academic honor held by KWC students, "The Order of Oak and Ivy," plus became a two-time All-American and three-time NCAA College Division Championship. From graduating in May 1969, success has defined George Tinsley for seven decades.

—Roy Pickerill

Sports Information Director Emeritus and Special Assistant For College Relations

Kentucky Wesleyan College

Mr. George Tinsley, Sr. (fondly known as Mr. T to those he mentors and inspires) is a resonating reminder that lasting success can be acquired by turning obstacles into opportunities. His origin story is the true original recipe for all who desire to translate their dreams into realities. Mr. T embodies the consummate teammate and professional. No matter the industry or playing field, his mindset and unyielding integrity are invaluable blueprints for the driven businessman/businesswoman and devoted family man. Inscribed within the chapters of the book you will find the details of what truly set him apart from the common business mogul. It is his willingness to share his wealth of knowledge. Through his commitment to excellence and well-rounded achievements, he enriches the lives of those in his local community and global business network. Mr. T—thank you for blazing the trial.

—B.Rich
Brandon Richard

The B.Rich Project, Inc.

George Tinsley, Sr. is an embodiment of inspiration. His resilience, entrepreneurial genius, and unwavering commitment to the community has not only shaped his success but the success of countless others. He is a beacon of hope and determination, and he infuses that spirit in others, all while helping to unleash their potential to achieve their dreams and goals. He is in the business of empowering and building leaders through his numerous entrepreneurial endeavors. His life story is a testament to the power of perseverance and visionary leadership.

—Lakecia Gunter

George Tinsley, Sr. demonstrates what shining triumphs are possible—if we have the courage to believe in ourselves and our dreams. His loving commitment to family, unflappable demeanor, and innate dignity have inspired future leaders everywhere. Many will live more fulfilling lives by following his example.

—Terrian Barnes

George Tinsley, Sr. is a shining example of a man who remembers where he came from, knows exactly where he's going, loves his family without condition, turns forbidding obstacles into golden opportunities, and always makes time to reach back and teach others how to succeed; not just in business, but in life.

—Ronald J. Gomes
(retired) Vice President, Strategic Alliances

George Tinsley Sr. is an inspiring figure who embodies resilience, exudes empathy, and conducts himself at all times with grace and dignity. Despite overwhelming odds, he was able to focus on core values and unconditional love while keeping a positive attitude. This has resulted in undeniable success, inspiring those wanting to go higher and farther; be it athletics, business, or, most importantly, putting family and friendship first.

—Donny MacKenzie

Executive Director

FFLA, Funding Florida Legal Aid

The immensely inspiring life story of George Tinsley, Sr. is filled with life lessons that anyone would be well served to follow. We must all play the cards we are dealt in life as best we can, and many of us begin with a poor hand. But attitude, heart, commitment, determination, and a relentlessly positive attitude can make it possible to rise to success in life from the most difficult of circumstances and to thrive not only in business but in being a good and decent person who makes their community and those within it better. This incredible but true story proves it. Everyone who reads this book should profit from George's extraordinary example and be inspired to become better versions of themselves.

—Stephen R. Senn

Peterson & Myers, P.A.
225 East Lemon Street, Suite 300
Post Office Box 24628
Lakeland, Florida 33802-4628

HMSHost George Tinsley's latest book is a testament to his profound insight and unwavering commitment to excellence. His unique stories and perspectives enlighten and inspire, making this a must-read for anyone seeking to navigate life and business challenges to achieve their dreams.

—Michael A. Stephens
General Counsel & EVP of Legal Affairs

Hillsborough County Aviation Authority

George Tinsley, Sr. is an inspirational figure who embodies resilience and fortitude. Despite adversity in his life, he has succeeded and become a beacon of hope for many aspiring entrepreneurs. George is a true leader whose impact is profound, transformative, and highly motivating.

—Michael Price
Senior Vice President

HMSHost by Avolta

I have known George Tinsley for many years. He is a very impressive gentleman who has overcome adversity and become a successful business owner and a great family man. He is a true leader whose impact is profound, transformative, and highly motivating. He has inspired many to become successful in business and their own personal lives.

—Barney Barnett

George is a very polished individual and a captivating speaker with a contagious smile. He and Seretha have been blessed with amazing leadership skills and a strong work ethic. George positively influences everyone he meets. His book is heartwarming and very inspirational. You won't be able to put it down.

—Evan S. Pinther

How do you create a superstar who gives back? Do such individuals actually exist? Are rags-to-riches stories really true? All of that is answered inside this incredible story of poverty, abandonment, compassion, and hope. If you've ever struggled, saw your dreams dissolve, been told to quit, because you're not good enough, and think your story is over, read about this amazing athlete, entrepreneur, and philanthropist, who overcame it all, lived the dream, and continuously gives back. Those of us who are lucky enough to know the man and his generous family can tell you that he lives it every day. For underdogs everywhere, devour this book!

—Stephen Giordano
President and CEO

Boys & Girls Clubs of Polk County

I have known George Tinsley for over forty years. I have watched his professional development as he moved from his early days at KFC as a manager to a multi-unit supervisor to a KFC franchisee. That was only the beginning, and he has built his businesses as a multi-franchise operator and more. George has always had a positive attitude and strong work ethic. He has worked hard for his success, and it is wonderful that he is sharing what he learned with others.

—Don Parkinson

Winner! Two words define that declaration: George Tinsley. His is a success story lived by a child raised in a home without either a mother or a father present. George did not even learn his real last name until his sophomore year in college. Here is a "don't shoot" freshman college basketball player who finished his career with over 1,000 points, first-team All-American, three NCAA D2 Championships, and Tourney MVP in his senior year. He became a pro player in the ABA. Upon his retirement, George joined the business world, first with KFC. George later branched into the fast-food business on his own. He overcame a fire that destroyed his restaurant, but George purchased a van and took food to the people. This became a national trend. George W. Tinsley, Sr. was on his way to the top! This is how you define a winner! George Tinsley.

—Joel Utley
KY Wesleyan Broadcaster, 61 years (ret)

Over the more than twenty-five years I have known George Tinsley, Sr., he has consistently embodied positivity and inspiration. His resilience, entrepreneurial genius, and unwavering commitment to the community have shaped his success and motivated countless others. George has mentored numerous individuals personally and professionally over the years and has been an enabler for them to have very successful careers and families! He is a beacon of hope and determination, and his life story and innumerable accomplishments are a testament to the power of perseverance and visionary leadership.

—Jeff Yablum

CEO/Owner

Cedar Tree Restaurant Group, LLC

George Tinsley has been a friend of mine since our high school days. We have developed a friendship that has become a true brotherly love. George has utilized his talents through the years to become one of the most renowned businessmen in his profession. I have witnessed his successful growth and development, willingness to share, and determination to give back to others who want to show his commitment to a successful lifestyle. His life story is a purpose-driven challenge to be the best and prove to others that obstacles can indeed be opportunities for achievement.

—Garnett Phelps

George Tinsley's life story is truly inspirational. What makes Mr. Tinsley's story unique—he actually "Talks the Talk," but he also "Walks the Walk." His principles in living will strengthen your foundation and calibrate your moral compass. His story will leave your soul with an enduring positive imprint.

Many successful people enjoy helping others learn life lessons to help us navigate this world with less of the bumps and bruises that life can bring. George W. Tinsley is a successful person who gives back so much to his communities and the people around him.

But George does not just give you advice; he lives his advice daily. His foundation is so strong that he weathers any storm and moves everyone toward their goals.

He follows his moral compass and rarely has a day that he does not positively impact someone around him. I have witnessed George in challenging business situations, and his ability to glean the positive out of any trauma is genuinely astounding. I have been fortunate enough to work with many successful people and can genuinely say George's life is inspirational.

—Howard Beckert

George Tinsley, Sr. is an inspiring figure who embodies resilience. Despite adversity, he has succeeded and become a beacon of hope for many aspiring entrepreneurs. George is a true leader whose impact is profound, transformative, and highly motivating.

—Bud Coleman
Retired

George Tinsley, Sr. is an embodiment of inspiration. His keen ability to turn obstacles into opportunities shows resiliency and entrepreneurial genius. His commitment to the community has shaped his success and motivated countless others. He is an invaluable asset to anyone seeking excellence in life.

—Brandon Giles

It is a privilege and pleasure to write this testimonial for George Tinsley, Sr. He epitomizes a person who has achieved the "American Dream," going from poverty to a wealthy entrepreneur and civic leader.

He gives back to society in many ways. His motivational speaking empowers his subjects to achieve maximum levels by utilizing his basic creed of faith, family, and friends. George utilizes his intellect, self-discipline, and integrity to make the extraordinary seem normal.

He is an American legend!

—Coach Guy Strong

CATCH AS CATCH CAN

GEORGE TINSLEY, SR.

CATCH AS CATCH CAN

BUILDING A LEGACY BY FINDING
OPPORTUNITY IN EVERY OBSTACLE

Advantage | Books

Published by Advantage Books, Charleston, South Carolina.
An imprint of Advantage Media.

ADVANTAGE is a registered trademark, and the Advantage colophon is a trademark of Advantage Media Group, Inc.

Printed in the United States of America.

10 9 8 7 6 5 4 3 2 1

ISBN: 978-1-64225-842-4 (Paperback)
ISBN: 978-1-64225-841-7 (eBook)

Library of Congress Control Number: 2024907391

Cover design by Analisa Smith.
Layout design by Ruthie Wood.

This publication is designed to provide accurate and authoritative information in regard to the subject matter covered. It is sold with the understanding that the publisher is not engaged in rendering legal, accounting, or other professional services. If legal advice or other expert assistance is required, the services of a competent professional person should be sought.

Advantage Books is an imprint of Advantage Media Group. Advantage Media helps busy entrepreneurs, CEOs, and leaders write and publish a book to grow their business and become the authority in their field. Advantage authors comprise an exclusive community of industry professionals, idea-makers, and thought leaders. For more information go to **advantagemedia.com**.

To my adoptive mother, Willie Tinsley, "Momma," who raised and took care of me for thirteen years of my formative years.

To Mary Johnson, my sister, who was my rock as I grew up and who was always there supporting me.

To my wife of fifty-two years, who has been there through all of my successes and has been a very intricate part of that success.

To my son, George II, who has played an enormous part in our success.

To Clarence and Olivia Tinsley, for raising me from thirteen years old through graduation from Kentucky Wesleyan College.

To Coach Guy Strong for offering me an opportunity to receive a full college scholarship to play basketball at Kentucky Wesleyan College in 1966.

To my biological mother, Fannie Gowdy Penebaker Tucker, for bringing me into this world.

To my biological father, Theodore William Penebaker, for bringing me into this world.

To my seventh grade school teacher, Mrs. Gaye Howell, who helped change my self-esteem to believing that I could achieve my goals and dreams.

CONTENTS

CHAPTER ONE

GROWING UP

I remember every detail of that small room in our Louisville house: the double-sized bed in one corner against the wall, the piled-up brown cardboard boxes containing all my clothes and belongings, and the small window next to the bed with our only view to the outside world. In another corner was a kitchenette with a gas stove, refrigerator, pots, and pans. This room was home to Mama and me for many of my formative childhood years.

It was situated in the back of a boarding house on Walnut Street in the heart of Louisville's East End. We ate there and hung out there, listening to the radio. We slept in the same bed. We had to go outside to the courtyard for running water or to the front of the complex to use the bathroom. It was a large brick building, with multiple rooms that were rented out to others. The lady who owned the building lived in the front with her daughters, son, and grandchildren.

There was one stand-alone two-bedroom home in the rear that faced the alley. Webb's Meat Market, owned by a white family, was the neighborhood store where we got our produce and other necessities.

My very first job, at age eleven, was at a chicken processing plant on Wenzel Street, earning five cents an hour.

Mama and I lived in similar places until I was thirteen. Her name was Willie Tinsley, and despite having different last names, she was Mama to me—the only mother I knew. She was short, dark-skinned, with a medium build and gray hair worn in plats. For as long as I could remember, her health was frail. She hobbled around on one leg and a crutch, but she was always good-natured.

Over the years, Mama and I grew used to survival mode, shuttling from one cramped living space to the next. First was a small dwelling on 19th and Chestnut in the west of Louisville. Next was a move to Harrods Creek just outside of Louisville to live with Mama's relatives. From there came quarters in the East End Gray Street to start elementary school, then to East Walnut Street, and later to Smoketown. Back then, those neighborhoods were primarily low-income African American communities with a sprinkling of white residents.

We relied mainly on Mama's sixty-five-dollar monthly social security check for food and everything else. I'd go to Webb's and, using Mama's account, get fruit and vegetables, canned goods, and whatever else the household needed. Mama would then make our meals—mostly basic soups of vegetables, maybe chicken, hot-water cornbread, and crackling bread. We'd stretch those meals out over several days. At night, I usually washed whatever clothes I wore that day, hung them out to dry, and put them back on the next day.

A FLASHBACK MOMENT

More than sixty years later, as I stood on the back lawn of my family home in Florida, my thoughts took me back to that room. I was a world away by then, living with Seretha, my wife of over fifty-one years, in our sprawling lakefront home in an upscale section of Winter Haven, Florida. My son, George II, a wonderful, accomplished man in his forties, resided next door.

We were hosting a gathering of my family—my wife, son, and a big extended circle of relatives and close friends. Having these loved ones close together brought on the stark reflection of my childhood home and the life I had with Mama.

The occasion was the celebration of life for my precious daughter, Penni, who had passed a year earlier. The untimely loss of my daughter at age forty-three from multiple system atrophy—a Parkinson's-like nerve degenerating disease—had devastated me. I'd been her primary caregiver for the last three years of her life, and that period allowed me to express my love for her in her time of most profound need.

This get-together in Penni's honor also gave me pause to reflect on my life. We had held back from hosting the event through the challenging first period of the COVID-19 pandemic. Now the celebration was on with all her close friends and family all together reflecting on their relationship with Penni. Three hundred–plus people came for the occasion, some from as far off as Kentucky, California, the Carolinas, New Jersey, and New York.

We pitched a massive white tent on the back lawn near our lake to accommodate the crowd. One thing hit me hard as I greeted the visitors: no one from Mama's family or my sister Mary's family, the folks who raised me, who had formed my world back in Louisville, was there. The lingering COVID-19 pandemic and probably the travel cost prevented some of them from coming.

Perhaps their absences brought a flashback to the place I had called home for many of my formative years, and the close-knit circle of the family who formed my world. I'd experienced so many pivotal moments since then—navigating through college, learning the ins and outs of life as a professional basketball player, marrying the woman of my dreams, and building a significant business franchise from scratch. My thoughts about the room where Mama and I lived brought on ideas of other key scenes in my early life.

THE MOUSE ATTACK

One particularly stark flashback was the night a mouse ran up the wall beside our bed. It jumped with a thump on the mattress and scampered across me to the other side where Mama was sleeping. As I jerked awake in shock and let go of a yell, it bit Mama on the arm. And then, just like that, it was gone.

Despite our hardscrabble existence, this middle-of-the-night episode shocked me. Fearing infection, we knew we had to move fast to ensure Mama would be all right. We dressed quickly and walked the two miles in the dark to Louisville General Hospital Clinic. I stayed close while Mama received a checkup and a shot.

The back and forth, the long wait, and the consultation took hours. As the night wore into the morning, questions were swirling in my mind. *What would happen to me if Mama had to stay in the hospital? Who would take care of me if she fell seriously ill?*

Years later, I understood that it was not the mouse that kept the details crystal clear in my mind. It was the realization of what Mama and I meant to one another. She also had an adult son, Clarence, who was several years my senior and lived in Smoketown with his wife, Olivia. Mama also had an adopted adult daughter, Mary Johnson, who came over monthly, bringing warm cheer, support, and sometimes food. She was seventeen years older than me and as close and loving a big sister as I could ever want.

But both Clarence and Mary resided too far to be of any help in case of emergencies. Without a phone or easy access to transportation, we could not communicate immediately that we needed assistance. Whenever we needed anything, I had to run or walk to find Clarence in Smoketown.

DRESSING FOR SUCCESS

The broader lesson of that time—of what it meant to have a sense of family and the duties and joys that come along with that—is what has remained with me over the years. What I understood may have been common sense to most folks but seemed profound to my ten-year-old mind: it was ultimately just Mama and me in the world to look after one another. We were responsible for each other. Since then, my utter allegiance to the family has been one of the cornerstones of my life.

Now, all these years later, standing in my backyard in Florida, clad in custom-tailored attire, celebrating the life of my daughter, and gazing over my family, I was vividly reminded of that moment and the journey I traveled. Despite the recent loss of my daughter, I couldn't help but feel blessed for the time she was in my life, a precious gift from God.

Today, my wardrobe is much different from my upbringing. I now wear hand-tailored clothes, a significant upgrade from the hand-me-downs of my youth. This was a practice I started during my time as a professional athlete and continued during my days as a corporate professional.

With no money for clothes or shoes in my adolescence and early adulthood, everything I wore had been donations from the church or other charities. I was a big kid and grew rapidly. When I was in seventh grade, I was already six feet tall; by ninth grade, I was six-foot-four. By age thirteen, I wore size-twelve-and-a-half shoes.

Most of what I had to wear didn't fit appropriately. At a time when my schoolmates were socializing, I was embarrassed to show up at events. Whenever I was invited to a social event, I bowed out. Dating was not in the cards. That, in turn, put a big damper on my self-esteem. But I knew I had to find ways to maneuver through these kinds of obstacles, from the small stuff like clothing to the big stuff like learning Mama was not my birth mother.

But I am getting ahead of the story.

FACING CHALLENGES

From an early age, I had to learn how to face challenges head-on and turn them into opportunities.

Standing inside the tent in the rear of my Florida home, surrounded by my adoring family and loved ones, it was a logical moment to take mental stock of the fruits of my labor. Behind me was the 7,500-square-foot five-bedroom house I shared with Seretha, complete with a courtyard and pool. To this day, my son lives in a big house next door—our two homes spread across six acres.

I may look and live like a different man than my upbringing, but I have never forgotten my roots and hard knocks. Seretha and I have always focused on taking care of the most important things—creating a home and ensuring the kids received a good education and became good people.

As the president and CEO of Tinsley Family Concessions, I have been able to do just that. With a consortium of four companies, our reach is immense. We own and operate more than sixty restaurants, mainly in Miami, Tampa, and Louisville airports, such as

KFC, Chili's, Auntie Anne's, Shula's, PF Chang's, Pei Wei, Bourbon Academy & Tasting Room, Burger King, Pizza Hut, Starbucks, Home Team Sports Bar and Grill, and Nathan's Hot Dogs. We also own our Tinsley Family Corporate office complex, where the business is based, in Winter Haven, Florida.

We are highly invested in Winter Haven, Polk County, and communities that we do business in along with serving on multiple boards, and we also are part of a local church congregation called First Missionary Baptist Church. Seretha and our son George II are senior executives in the company, and we recently completed the transition of George II into the senior executive position of president. Several other relatives are among the employees.

I am pleased and humbled that the businesses have succeeded enough to afford us a decent life. And I confess to certain indulgences. Especially coming from a poor background, I have found it fun to allow myself little toys like custom suits and luxury vehicles. Seretha is the complete opposite, which makes us a perfect balance.

But, of course, our family is far more important than any material possessions we have amassed. Meeting the woman who would become my wife back in college was one of the greatest miracles of my life. We've been married for over five decades and have always been dedicated partners in everything we do. George II is all I could ever want in a son. He is a remarkable leader and poised to run the business. Since the passing of Penni, our family bonds have only tightened.

My family has come to include a broad group of relatives that I began connecting with in my youth. I have sixteen siblings, dozens of cousins, nieces, and nephews. I am also proud of the accomplishments of my sister Mary's children who have wonderful families. Her daughter Dr. Rana Johnson, PhD, has been extremely accomplished in the world of academia. She was very close to Penni during her early years. She is presently a VP at Kansas State University.

Seeing such a warm and loving family coming together to support Penni made me feel even more devoted to and responsible for my own family. As time has passed, this sentiment has only grown stronger, particularly as I reflect on the fact that it was almost taken away from me before it even began.

LIVING THROUGH RACIAL TENSION

I grew up in the racially charged 1950s and 1960s when tensions between African American and white citizens were flaring up across the South. Emmett Till was killed the year I was in fourth grade, 1955. He was a fourteen-year-old African American boy, not much older than myself at the time.

Hearing the news of how he had been abducted, tortured, and lynched in Mississippi after being accused of offending a white woman cast a stark reality over our African American communities nationwide, including our neighborhoods in Louisville, Kentucky. It reinforced the basic concerns of what we, as African Americans, should or should not do. We had to be aware of the need to be careful of our surroundings, particularly around white women, and in traveling in white-only neighborhoods. The threat of racial clashes was a big reason for caution.

As a kid, that meant being careful of who I was hanging out with and steering clear of trouble. Like any other kid, I got into my share of mischief, such as the afternoon I clumsily shot a BB gun toward a neighbor's window. But I never did anything intentionally wrong.

The streets where I lived in Louisville were not all mean, but there were groups and gangs that would take advantage of you or try to manipulate you to join them or get you in trouble.

There were certainly places and people to avoid, and I became adept at doing that. I needed to be there for Mama and could not afford to get in trouble. But in the era of Emmett Till's murder, an African American person didn't have to commit a crime to be accused of one.

DEVELOPING A SIXTH SENSE

The day I was apprehended by the police for theft, I was only eleven. It happened on a Saturday afternoon. From the doorway of the room I shared with Mama, I saw two police officers make their way through the alley behind our building and enter our courtyard. They were in uniform, armed, and white. The sight of these armed officers was startling. They had come looking for me.

Their questions came fast and furious. A bubble gum machine had been stolen from Webb Meat Grocery, the store down the block, and they had found the machine in the alley behind the store. Whoever stole it had taken the nickels, pennies, and other change inside.

"What do you know about this?" one of the officers asked.

"Were you at the store earlier today?" yelled the other.

I recognized one of the police officers as the store owner's son and told them the truth. "Yes," I answered. "But I don't know anything about any bubble gum machine."

I had stopped by Webb's that morning with two pals from the neighborhood. The three of us had decided to see if we could get summer jobs at the nearby stockyard and we popped into the store on the way there to get donuts and snacks. When the stockyard did not hire us, we went straight home. It wasn't an unusual trip, and I had never used the bubble gum machine. Besides, it was so heavy I couldn't have ever lifted it anyway.

My older sister, Mary, happened to come by when the cops arrived, and so she came out to the alley where they were demanding answers from me. The longer the conversation went, the more she grew incensed.

"My brother doesn't steal!" she told them. "You are questioning the wrong person. He would never do anything like that."

In retrospect, I think her intervention saved me. It was a scary encounter. I had heard stories of kids getting thrown into jail for minor offenses, and in that moment I thought I would get locked up and be accused of something I didn't do. I was terrified of becoming another statistic in the daunting number of incarcerated African American youth.

Eventually, the police officers determined I wasn't a criminal and let me go. To this day, whenever I return to Louisville and visit that area, I always stop at Webb's. Until a couple of years ago, the same family still owned the store, and the son, the police officer, took over the management. I liked going to remind them who I was and where I am today in my career. Even all these years later, I still remind them I didn't steal that machine.

That harrowing experience of being confronted by police would serve as a major life lesson to always navigate any situation—work, social, or otherwise—with caution. From then on, instinct became my primary guidance. I've always felt that I have a God-given sixth sense that keeps me away from negative people or situations. I've always been able to pick up on vibes that tell me, "This is not what you need to do" or "You're in an area where you don't need to be."

If people started drinking, especially if they were of a different race or background, I knew the whole atmosphere would change and recognized when it was time to move. My rule about being prudent at even the hint of trouble and being cautious also carried over to my years as a college and professional athlete. Many of my classmates and teammates sometimes yielded to temptations, but I never did. Without that God-given sixth sense, and without the way Mama raised me in the church, I don't know where I would be today.

GOD IN MY CORNER

I have always felt God looking out for me, and that altercation with the cops was just one example. That following Christmas season when I was eleven, I remember Mama and I had no means to have any celebration. While kids in our neighborhood were discussing the gifts they wanted to get, I pulled back from those conversations.

If Mama and I received anything at Christmas, it was from Green Street Baptist Church. My sister Mary would also try to do what she could, but she had children of her own and did not have a regular job. The monthly check Mama got always went quicker than a popsicle in August. We were resigned to spending Christmas like any other day, with a bowl of soup and a prayer. I visited with some of my closest friends in the neighborhood and shared their family fun.

But one year, as Christmas neared, I was walking from home down Walnut Street when I looked down and behold, I found twenty dollars lying on the sidewalk! I had to do a double take, but it was real. That provided the means for a gift both for Mama and for me. Miraculously, the same thing happened at Christmas the following year. Again, I found twenty dollars on the sidewalk, this time on

Broadway near the animal hospital. And that unexpected gift allowed us a small measure of holiday cheer.

Given the timing and the circumstances, finding money during the Christmas holidays could not have been a coincidence. There was only one explanation: God was looking out for me. Today, as I move around, I always carry a twenty-dollar bill to give away to the needy on the street when they approach me. It is my way of giving back God's blessings.

One of the greatest gifts Mama gave me was appreciating the importance of faith and worship. She was a very religious person and loved God. She often sat next to our big radio and listened to *Church*, featuring Reverend Ike and his Prayer Cloth influence. The African American radio evangelist used his broadcasts to preach the gospel of money and well-being. Mama believed in his message and would shout and cry during his programs. In quieter moments, she would talk to me about my spiritual life. Over time, her lessons resonated.

Church was an essential part of my life. When I was a kid, I joined Green Street Baptist. The minister, Reverend J. V. Bottoms, Sr., was an influential figure and a community role model. African Americans from all over Louisville worshiped there. When Reverend Martin Luther King visited Louisville, he came to the church to visit. It would become my religious touchstone, my church home.

My grade school friends all went there, and it's where my first friendships developed. There was just a lot of culture for me that was centered there. While I was not there every Sunday, my monthly attendance during school and my professional sports career was particularly impactful.

Our involvement in the church and living with Mama taught me not only spiritual rules to live by but life lessons as well. Even as an adolescent, it was my job to help manage the household. Mama couldn't read, so to pay our bills and purchase food, she'd make an X, and I'd sign her name.

I had to juggle the food budget, making adjustments along the way. While most kids were out playing ball, I was figuring out how to make ends meet. I had free lunch tickets in school, and I did a lot of side-hustle jobs around the neighborhood to make some spare change. In those days, when I visited close friends, their parents would sometimes offer me food to eat. Neighborhoods were close and on occasion families would share when things were going well.

One of the hustles that came on later was selling pies. Mama's adult son Clarence worked at the Blue Bird Pie Company in Smoketown, and he knew I liked the small pies the business made. He'd bring some home for the family and give some to me. Whenever I passed by the company, one of his work colleagues, whom I called Uncle Zack, would also give me pies here and there. I think everyone in Smoketown had at least one Blue Bird Pie at one time or another.

They did not know that I would sell the pies to friends at school. They were five- or ten-cent pies, and I would sell them for fifteen. Somewhere in there, my entrepreneurial spirit was born. Throughout those early years of hustling, of learning survival skills and putting them to use, whether I deserved it or not, it became clear that some higher power was in my corner, fighting for me.

GEORGE WILLIAM TINSLEY

I needed God on my side more than ever when I was thirteen and three other impressionable incidents occurred in short order. Although I did not know it then, those experiences influenced me heavily as I defined who I was and processed what inspired and motivated me.

The first was a move from the room on Louisville's East End where Mama and I had been living to Smoketown, a well-known African American community. At seventy-eight, Mama's health was deteriorating, and she was becoming bedridden. She first went for an extended stay in a hospital. While she was there, I moved in with Clarence and his wife Olivia into their apartment, which consisted of one bedroom and a kitchenette.

The new home base was a step up. Smoketown was a vibrant neighborhood. It had been Louisville's most prominent and best-known African American stronghold for decades. Many neighbors were teachers, deacons, mailmen, coaches, and educators. They would become role models to me. Ballard Park, an ample open green space close to the new place, was a neighborhood sports and recreation park that was my new stomping ground, a welcome retreat, and a springboard for my athletic career.

But as always, there were challenges. Clarence, then in his thirties, worked at night, while Olivia had a day job. Because of his odd hours and the small size of the apartment, Olivia and I ended up having to share the bed. Neither of us was happy about that arrangement. Eventually, while Mama was still in the hospital, we moved to a house located at 908 South Jackson Street. This time we had two bedrooms, a living room, a kitchen, and a bathroom. When Mama came home from the hospital, I shared a bed with her once again.

One fall afternoon gave way to the second event. Mama's check came. I cashed it, and she gave me the money to get a pair of Chuck Taylor All-Star shoes at a pawn shop on Preston Street, near the house. The Chuck Taylor All-Stars were my shoe of choice in those days. I went through a pair about every month. The shop's closest size was eleven, a size and a half too small. But I bought them and made them fit.

On one of these trips to the store, I returned home, excited about my purchase, and went to Mama's room, only to find her asleep.

"Mama, look what I got," I said.

She didn't answer.

I ran into the other room and woke up Clarence, who was sleeping before his night shift.

"There's something wrong with Mama," I said. "She's not waking up."

Clarence got up, walked into Mama's room, and also failed to wake her.

"Well, the old girl's gone," he finally said. With that, he just turned around and walked away.

My world was rocked. I cried and cried. To make matters worse, no one else seemed to have that same concern or feeling. I couldn't understand why. Over the next few weeks, I went through the stages of grief. As I passed from denial to acceptance that Mama was gone, I began to worry about what would happen to me. It was evident that I was invading the privacy and lives of Clarence and his wife, but they allowed me to continue to stay in the house.

Shortly after Mama's death, Aunt Louise Taylor, a relative and the matriarch of the family who lived in Harrods Creek where we lived for four years, came to take care of the funeral arrangements. That's when I experienced yet another life-altering event. At one point, she asked me how I wanted to be listed on the funeral program. She also asked what name she should use. Both questions stunned me.

When I first entered school, I was listed on the class rosters as George Wm. Penebaker. As a kid, I was not sure of the origin of that name, only that I was told it was on my birth certificate, which I had never actually seen. But as I settled into the school and the larger

East End neighborhood, everybody else adapted to using Tinsley. The name Penebaker had not entered my mind for years.

Her questioning, in turn, led me to search for my birth certificate. To my shock, for the first time in years, I realized once again that my given family name was Penebaker, but more shockingly, I learned again that Mama wasn't my biological mother, and Clarence and Mary weren't my birth siblings.

My birthdate that I had been celebrating, per the birth certificate, was wrong. My birthday was actually September 19, while I had been told it was September 27. As the years passed, the reality of who I was would be buried deep in the back of my mind unless some traumatic event triggered the reminder that I was adopted by Mama.

As those facts crystallized, they drove home that I didn't biologically belong to that family, even though they had raised me. And now Mama, the one who cared for me most of those years, was gone. The only close bond I had left was Mary. Even though I called her sister, it seemed that everything I had come to know about my family was not legally valid.

That was perhaps my most transformative period, one of soul-searching and personal despair. It required me to ask tough questions: *Who am I? Who do I belong to? Who were my birth parents? What happened to them?* These questions passed for the time. Clarence and Olivia provided a home, and Clarence from time to time (when drinking) indicated that he could be my father given he dated my mother. Mary always, without question, took up the responsibility of making sure I was OK and loved as her baby brother after Mama's passing.

As I explored these questions to their depths, it struck me, finally, that I was not in a bad place. I had the cornerstones that Mama had raised me on and that I had already begun to hone, such as my allegiance to family. Even though I knew many kids who had been raised by single moms, I had a burning desire to know who my real family was. But also, I knew I needed to navigate the world with caution. I understood that a higher power was watching over me. And I recognized the desire to be a successful spirit deep inside. I had the will to create a better world for myself.

There were still significant life issues for me to address. I was entering Louisville Male High School, a prominent high school in Louisville. *Would I graduate high school, which no one else in my family had achieved? Would I go to college and participate in college sports? Would I play professional basketball? Was I ultimately an entrepreneur or a family man?* I would have to work through that.

But even as a teenager, I had begun to create my world. The road to the building and flourishing of Tinsley Family Enterprises would be long and winding. The journey to building my family would be equally adventurous. But already, the foundations for both pursuits were laid. They started with my understanding of my identity. If anybody asked, I readily told them, "I am George William Tinsley."

To me, it was more than just a name. It represented the life lessons I had learned along the way. It was the name that Mama gave me and the love, sacrifices, dedication, and spirit she left me with. Perhaps most of all, it meant acknowledging and embracing my gift of turning challenges into opportunities as she had done over the thirteen years she dedicated to my upbringing.

CHAPTER TWO

"YOU SHOULD QUIT"

"George," Mrs. Warren said, "Can I speak with you about something?"

It was the first time my sixth-grade teacher had singled me out for a conversation, and my heart jumped as I walked toward her desk. My footsteps creaked on the floor with every step, and my heart thumped. *Was I being thrown out of school? Had someone complained about something I did or said?*

Classroom learning was never my strong suit. While I loved gaining knowledge about new things, I found it tough to find my way through books and tests. I didn't flunk any classes, but didn't ace any either and was resigned to life as a C student.

Nicholas Finzer School was a challenging environment for me. Due to Louisville's school desegregation program in the early 1950s, I was transferred to this school in my last couple of elementary school years. Before that, I had studied at Frederick Douglas School in the East End of Louisville. However, when this all-Black school closed in 1954, I was transferred to Nicholas Finzer, which was a three-story brick building located on the corner of Broadway and Shelby Streets. The school had an all-white faculty and a predominantly white student body, and I was now studying in Mrs. Warren's sixth-grade class after completing my first two years there.

When I look back on that era, it occurs to me that many of the Finzer students and teachers had become accustomed to the segregated culture of the school—and of Louisville in general. With the sudden influx of Black kids in classes, teachers were apparently uncomfortable with the culture change and uncertain how to fit this new set of students into their curriculum.

As it turned out, the reason Mrs. Warren summoned me was not one of those fears that ran through my head as I approached her desk. It was something worse. She looked me straight in the eyes. In her late fifties, she was stern, short, with dark hair that she wore in a ponytail. A veteran teacher, Mrs. Warren had a reputation as blunt-spoken, and in my months in her class, she had lived up to it.

"George, why don't you just quit school," she said. "You're not doing well. You're not going to make it."

For a thirteen-year-old struggling to find my place in a complex and changing world, those words stung worse than wasp bites across my face. In a culture where adolescents respected the perspective of adults, I couldn't ignore her message. Neither could my classmates. She had talked loud enough for some of them to overhear. And yet, I didn't know how to respond. I just smiled and slumped back to my wooden seat near the back of the classroom.

I WON'T DROP OUT

For many students, moments like these marked the beginning of the end of formal education. Black kids often hang on to school by a thread. For many Blacks who, like me, were swept from a familiar community school to one populated chiefly by strangers, the desegregation era was unnerving. I knew of a lot of my peers who just couldn't deal with the dramatic transition from all-Black schools where everybody knew everybody to primarily white schools where there was no emotional support. They just dropped out to work or support their families.

It was a national trend that would become more pronounced throughout the 1950s and 1960s. In 1967, a pivotal year for school desegregation, nearly one out of every three Black American kids had given up on formal education before finishing high school. Chances were this would be my story as well, and I could have easily slipped into the streets and become one of those statistics.

I didn't have much outside inspiration for my education. At home, Mama did not check my grades or homework. I didn't have anybody who said, "Hey, you need to go read this book. You need to do this." I would never classify myself as poor, dumb, or a below-average learner. I was just not motivated. I also didn't have the proper study habits.

Mama supported my schooling, but she couldn't read or write. So, all my education took place right there in the school building. Throughout my four years at Frederick Douglas, I maintained a low profile. All the students and teachers there came from the nearby Black community in the East End of Louisville.

Despite the atmosphere of familiarity, I had insecurities about my appearance, hand-me-down wardrobe, and home situation. I tried as much as I could to avoid the spotlight. When I had to show up, my coping mechanism was to become a kind of class clown. That status as a jokester lowered expectations for me to perform academically.

At Nicholas Finzer, there was no tolerance for that kind of behavior. Much taller than my classmates and with an awkwardly shaped head, I stood out. The teachers and other school authorities did not know what to make of me.

They had already held me back a grade. I finished fourth grade at Frederick Douglas. When I started at Finzer, I had to take a test. They also gave me a form to take home to have signed. Mama put an X on it, and I signed her name and took it back. Surprisingly, that process led to my placement in a class that combined fourth and fifth grades. It was a special section they designed for fifth graders they considered slow learners or students not prepared for the school's fifth-grade curriculum. It was one of many untrusting situations I experienced during my school years.

That afternoon, after Mrs. Warren suggested leaving school, I sat in the classroom, waiting for the period to end. Thoughts rushed through my head. The scene had rocked me to the core. It let me know that what I had been doing wasn't working. I had to do something different. At the time, I didn't know what new path to take. The obstacle before me was clear, but I did not yet know how to turn it into an opportunity. Still, I knew one thing: I would *not* drop out of school.

A TALE OF TWO TEACHERS

June 4, 1965, was a glorious occasion. On the evening of that early summer day, I graduated from Louisville Male High School. I walked across the stage at Freedom Hall in the Kentucky State Fairgrounds, where the ceremony was held, and the school principal handed me a diploma. A cheer rose from the crowd, and it was a euphoric moment.

Seven years had passed since Mrs. Warren suggested I drop out of school. In the years going forward, I would set high goals for myself and accomplish many of them. But finishing high school was my finest hour at that stage of my life. It represented a personal best on many levels.

For one, I was the first in my family to achieve that level of education. Besides the diploma, I received several other honors during the graduation ceremony. These included citations for achievements in basketball, cross-country, and track. The announcer also cited my admission to Kentucky Wesleyan College on a full athletic scholarship. I had received my draft notice, but service in the military would be deferred so I could further my education.

My sister Mary Johnson, her son Larry, and Olivia Tinsley attended the ceremony and stood by my side. After the ceremony, I lingered with some of my graduating pals and their families. Mary, Olivia, Aunt Louise, and I also huddled to celebrate. Standing there, I felt the warmth of family, belonging, and accomplishment I had often missed.

Above all, receiving my high school diploma validated my ability to overcome the odds. Since that afternoon when I was encouraged to drop out of school, I had worked diligently to prove I was worthy of an education. Once again, I had found a way to turn an obstacle into an opportunity.

Amid my euphoric graduation day, I reflected on my elementary school years, as I now had a better perspective on the dynamics of Nicholas Finzer and what had happened to me there. That was the early era of desegregation in a racially divided city in the southern United States. Desegregation posed dilemmas for Black and white teachers and students. The white teachers had to digest a lot that was new. They had to learn how to interact with the new Black students, process and deal with their different behavioral patterns, and other things going on in their homes.

For an older generation of white teachers like Mrs. Warren, there was a disconnect that presumed Black students were behaviorally challenged. She just seemed to assume negative behavior and lacked the ability to empathize. The fact that we were together all day in the same classroom only made the situation worse. We could go to lunch or recreation, but after that, we'd be back in that same room with that same teacher the whole day.

As a result, I was under the constant scrutiny of a teacher who was not seeing me. And in my early adolescent years, I wasn't the best version of myself. I wasn't the best dressed. And my self-esteem was very low.

Without strong external influences, I knew I had to find a better way to approach school and life. The only path forward was for me to start digging deeper into what skills I had, to study harder, and to apply myself. That can-do attitude helped me through Mrs. Warren's class and finish at Nicholas Finzer. And coupled with a new dynamic at my following schools, it motivated me through junior high and high school.

I have always looked internally for my drive and motivation, setting my own goals based on what I wanted to do. Since I was lacking a big brother or any other real role model who was participating in sports or student activities, I didn't have that challenge to actually get involved. I had to look deep inside at my own human resources.

Yet, I did not have to forge the road through school alone. Starting with my first year of junior high school at Eastern Junior High School, throughout my teenage years and into college, I had the support of remarkable teachers, coaches, spiritual leaders, and friends and families from the community. The first was Ms. Howell, my seventh-grade homeroom and social studies teacher. She became an impactful mentor and a positive force in my life.

She was in every way a contrast from Mrs. Warren. Ms. Howell was short and dark-haired, a recent college grad who was in her twenties. She had a warm, welcoming presence and an empathic approach to the students. From the moment we encountered one another, she saw something positive in me and took an interest in nurturing it.

A keen observer, Ms. Howell watched how I maneuvered through the school environment. Given that she was my homeroom teacher, she knew I had tickets for a free lunch but didn't use them. Maybe she understood that I knew the other kids would see I was on a free school lunch program and tease me about it. Instead, I would go to the gym and play.

She took me under her wing and started bringing me bananas, apples, and sandwiches. She encouraged me to do better. But the pivotal event came when Ms. Howell offered me the job as "projector boy." I became the go-to guy to set up projectors whenever anyone wanted to watch a movie. Being the projector guy was a big responsibility in a school where watching films was wildly popular.

Ms. Howell likely considered it a hands-on task that would motivate me. If so, her thinking was spot on. I took the job and the responsibilities that came with it to heart. This job gave me confidence and self-esteem and with time, I worked harder to learn new things. I also worked to improve my whole approach to learning. Bit by bit, I became more accepted and identified.

BASKETBALL

In my adolescent world, an ounce of self-confidence seemed to flow like a river. With just a bit of self-esteem, I developed a better sense of how to perform in the classroom. As I progressed through junior high, my thinking and motivation about academia underwent a positive transformation. I learned how to interact with different types of teachers and to understand what they were looking for from me—particularly with the younger teachers.

I created a bond with every teacher I had in their twenties. It seemed like they understood us Black kids and were more sensitive to our situations. Those positive experiences, in turn, inspired me to elevate my grades. I performed best in typing, science, health, physical education, and Spanish classes. English and math were more of a struggle, and I was still mostly a C student. But slowly, ever so slowly, I began to make As and Bs!

My achievements in sports also played a pivotal role in lifting my sense of self-worth. While in the classrooms, I wanted to blend into the woodwork; on the fields and courts, I was challenged by coaches to achieve excellence. I fell in love with competition in fifth grade while living in the East End of Louisville with Mama. There was no TV, so my pastime became hanging out with friends at basketball courts and the park.

I didn't intend to become a basketball player. The sport came to me naturally. Being taller than my friends, I had a good balance of quickness and jumping ability. As a kid, I showed some potential on the court, and I was fulfilling a gap in my community. At that age, there was nobody who was exceptionally better than me in basketball, although there were some great track guys and terrific boxers.

That was the period that Cassius Clay, later to be known as Muhammad Ali, boxed on television, winning the Golden Gloves and then becoming an Olympic champion. He was from Louisville, and he worked out in Smoketown and the East End areas. I tried boxing, but that did not work out well, and therefore basketball, track, football, and softball were my sports of choice.

At first, I was awkward and didn't have the competitive mentality to be the best. I just wanted to be a part of the team and would rather pass than look for my shot. During my time in junior high school, my relationship with basketball took a different turn. Some coaches and players encouraged me to try out for the team and I found my niche as a defensive player and rebounder. Scoring points was not my strong suit, but I played a pivotal role as a team player.

Then, in my eighth-grade year, when we moved to Smoketown, my basketball experience shifted to a higher level. The players there were a sharper mix, including older guys, some of whom gambled on games. There was a heightened mood of competition and within that competitive world is where players gained their reputation. We would play a game, and there was always the after-game talk about who was the best and this and that. Because of my jumping ability, I began to attract attention.

THE NEXT STEP

The next step in my career was either going to Louisville Male High School or Central High School. Guy Strong was the head coach at Male High and had recruited me while I was at Eastern Junior High School. Prior to me attending Louisville Male High, he moved to Kentucky Wesleyan College and became head basketball coach there. There was a Black recruiter by the name of Bill Turner who recruited in Smoketown for Male. He scoped out who was rising above the average in the basketball courts in our neighborhoods and his role was to let the high school programs know who was good at different sports or just an all-around athlete.

I started to get a reputation in those circles as a player to watch. When I went to Male High in tenth grade, I got more serious about sports. I wanted to play football but didn't make the team. The new basketball coach, who had replaced Guy Strong, was Gene Rhodes who had a reputation of focus on basketball, and he wanted me to stick to basketball. Still an avid runner, I fell back on track and joined the cross-country team in the track program. There I began to shine. I was number one in cross-country. During track season, which follows basketball season, I ran the quarter-mile and mile relays as my primary focus. I also ran the 880-yard run and filled in on other events.

But basketball became a bigger and bigger focus. Coach Rhodes was very disciplined and liked to scream and holler. I was not used to this, and it made me very nervous as a sophomore. Nonetheless, I made the starting five two or three games into the season during my sophomore year, thanks to my jumping, defensive abilities, and fundamental skills. In my junior year, I became a key player on the team, averaging about ten points and ten rebounds a game at the center position. We were the number one ranked team in the state of Kentucky for most of the year. This was the year that one of Kentucky's greatest high school players, Wes Unseld, was a senior at Seneca High School. We lost to Wes's team in the regional finals and they went on to win State. I started center on our teams all three years at Louisville Male High School.

The sense of camaraderie shared among athletes and friends within the Smoketown neighborhood served as a significant source of inspiration and motivation. Nestled on the nine-hundred block of South Jackson Street, a tight-knit community thrived, comprising individuals like Shelly, Bobby, and Wallace Floyd. Wallace, a dedicated trainer, resided just across the street. Bobby and Shelly, both distinguished athletes, along with Lamont Goldstein, an exemplary student and athlete, contributed to the vibrant community spirit. Lamont lived a few doors down, known for his academic excellence and athletic prowess, enhancing our collective camaraderie. Additionally, Carey Guess, another resident of the same street, brought his own legacy of athleticism to the neighborhood. An accomplished track star and a product of a well-respected family in Smoketown, Carey's presence added depth to the rich tapestry of support and encouragement that characterized our close-knit community.

There was a tough guy we used to call Buddy Boy. His real name was James Rutledge, and he always vowed to protect me if I ever needed any help. Lastly there were the three Jones brothers who played football and basketball, who lived directly across the street. Each one of the boys received scholarships to college in sports and academics, and they set the tone for the rest of us.

John A. Jones was a high school football All-American who won a scholarship to Indiana University. Joel Bolden, whom I met and became friends with in the fifth grade while living on Walnut Street, had also become a very good basketball player and was the same height as me. We were good friends and very competitive with each other on the basketball court. We later attended college together and graduated from KWC together as the first Black athletes to ever graduate from KWC.

Several blocks away from where Mama and I lived on Walnut Street, there was a white family, the Eisenbachs. Their house was right on the edge of the Black community on Shelby Street. The family included five or six brothers and sisters and soon we became close. As a family, they were always supportive, and we remained great friends. Even now, decades later, we remain in contact through social media. They call me their brother from another mother. The George family and the Board and Harris families, along with others in the East End, were also very close and supportive.

By the time I reached high school, as I focused more on sports, my friendships with teammates also became more competitive. I think, for example, of Dallas Thornton. He was the star of our high school basketball team. A year ahead of me, he was a junior when I was a sophomore. And then there was Ted Rose, who came in as a sophomore standout. Both of them could put the ball in the hole along with great jumping ability. They were all-around athletes and received more attention than I did during high school because of their natural abilities. I had to work harder to develop my game. I later found out that Dallas and I were both born the same year, month, and in the same hospital.

So, for a while, I was caught between two stars. But then, when Dallas graduated, I became a featured player in a more central role on the team. We had a great point guard, Garnett Phelps, who was also an All-American and the very first quarterback recruited by the University of Kentucky football team. We became friends and have been great friends for over six decades.

CHURCH

Throughout those years, the church was another primary source of inspiration. When Mama and I lived on Gray Street in Louisville, I started attending Green Street Baptist Church a block away. Although I was not there every Sunday, I was a regular attendant through my childhood and college years and pro basketball years until I left Louisville.

People in the church looked out for Mama and me with gifts and donations. The Greathouses were one particularly supportive family. They knew our situation and the mother became a strong female mentor to me. The Greathouse children, John and Delores, had been friends since elementary school at Frederick Douglas. Various deacons and clergy within the church also began to give me recognition and support, especially as my athletic career developed and I was in the news.

Deacon Henry Jones, one of the head deacons, lived right across the street from where we lived in Smoketown. He and his family paid very close attention to my progression in athletics and in life. Jones was a postman in the East End, so he knew almost everyone in the neighborhood. He was the one who made sure that during the church service when they called out folks who were accomplishing positive things in the community, my name was always mentioned.

Many Black women in the church and, more broadly, in the neighborhood also played supportive roles in my upbringing. From Sunday school teachers to my friends' moms, they seemed to go out of their way to be a positive image for me. We communicated well, and they offered advice. They would invite me to dinner, lunch, or a meal when their kids ate.

In retrospect, Mrs. Warren may have done me a favor. It was not likely her intent, but by telling me I would not make it in school, she forced me to dig deep and prove her wrong. With constant work, the guidance of a higher power, and the support of a village surrounding me, I pulled through.

During my junior high school and college years, after I began to find my footing, I made it a point to go visit Mrs. Warren back at Nicholas Finzer School. It was in keeping with a mission I have had to show her and other people who doubted me that I could be somebody and that I was better than they perceived me to be. As I've gotten older and more successful, I have always maintained contact with those who underestimated me. I wanted them to believe that if given positive motivation we all can succeed. That said, I have always done this in a way that was not offensive.

Nonetheless, I wanted to tell people like the teacher that told me to quit to be careful how they judged and treated people. You never know who you may need. Even with the passage of years, Mrs. Warren never warmed up. During my return visits to her classroom, she always greeted me with a puzzled look as to why I kept coming back. I wanted her to know that I graduated from high school, received a scholarship to college, won three NCAA Championships, toured Europe and Africa, represented the United States as a goodwill ambassador, was a two-time All-American, made the dean's list, won the Oak & Ivy Award, and graduated from college.

Fortunately, she was more the exception than the rule in my early years. I was lucky to have grown up in a village of positive people—neighbors, teachers, coaches, teammates, family members, and others—coming together to help propel me forward. As I entered the formative years of college, I continued to need the support of that village. More than that, I needed to draw on my resourcefulness.

The experience of being told to follow my own guidance and that of the Higher Power at an early age has left a lasting impact on me. It taught me to stay true to myself and to ignore anyone who tried to steer me off course, put me down, or make me feel inferior. Even when others tried to diminish me in later years, I remained steadfast in my belief in my own potential and mission. I would never quit.

CHAPTER THREE

COLLEGE STARDOM

Most athletes can pinpoint the moment they hit a career-changing stride. I'm not referring to the times they got pumped about a big play on the court. I mean a game or event when everything flowed together, elevating their skills to a level that exceeded even their wildest dreams.

Of course, even for the most talented sports figures, excelling requires a process that builds over time. For me, that process involved years of intense practice, constant work, great coaching, and, perhaps above all, sheer willpower. My moment came toward the end of my freshman year at college. I was a starting forward for the Kentucky Wesleyan basketball team as a freshman the entire year. We had an excellent season, and we were invited to play in the NCAA Division II playoffs for the championship.

We had battled through the regional playoffs and besting Akron 105-74 in the quarterfinals. We were then matched up against Southern Illinois who was one of the top-ranked teams in the nation. Our two teams played a very close and tough match throughout the game. We played the same five guys the entire game without any substitutes. My primary responsibilities were to play defense on their best inside player, rebound, and keep team chemistry going. Our team goal was to prevent Southern Illinois from making easy baskets. Even decades later I remember playing a key role in the victory where my performance was above my season average. I scored fifteen points, snagged ten rebounds, and held my man to seven points for the game. He was an All-American named George McNeil.

Perhaps because basketball was the only major sport at Kentucky Wesleyan, the campus provided us with an incredible fan base. And that night, our fellow students, the Owensboro community, faculty, and their families came out in full force. Although we were playing forty miles from home in Evansville, Indiana, the bleachers were packed with our supporters, not only from campus but from the town of Owensboro, where the college was based. There were even some folks from Louisville, where many of our families came from.

That night, with the pressure on the court and the constant cheers from Roberts Municipal Stadium, the energy and excitement started high and kept rising. And then, with fifteen seconds to go and the score tied, Sam Smith sank the final shot. When the buzzer came marking the end, we had won 54-51. This victory gave us, KWC Basketball, our first NCAA national championship ever. The stadium erupted.

It was a glorious moment for the team and the college. Winning that NCAA national Division II championship set in motion a remarkable run of events. As a show of acknowledgment, the US State Department invited our team to represent the United States of America as goodwill ambassadors traveling to Europe and Africa the following summer. We would appear as American Goodwill Ambassadors, put on training sessions, compete in exhibition games against the state's best players, and visit with American ambassadors and other leaders in each country in West Africa.

For the following three years, our KWC basketball Panthers continued to rack up achievements. In addition to winning the NCAA national championship in my freshman year, we also won the title in my junior and senior years. For three of my four college years, we were national champions.

The first NCAA victory also provided me with a big boost. It gave me a rush of fortune that would propel me through a tremendous start to the rest of my college career. With the inspiration of that event, I proceeded to achieve season after season of personal bests in basketball, academics, and social achievements. By the time I completed my senior year, I had compiled 2,014 career points for a 16.9 scoring average throughout 119 consecutive games. I also grabbed a school record of 1,115 career rebounds, averaging 9.4 per game, and had a 47.6 goal percentage from the field and 76.4 from the charity stripe.

JUST ME

I took my most significant strides on the court in my junior and senior years. In that period, my scoring averages jumped 50 percent and I was an All-American for two years in a row. I also became the first Black student to win the Oak & Ivy Award, a recognition of the combination of student body and academic success and representation of the college.

Following my junior year, I also received an invitation to participate in the 1968 US Olympic trials. They put together a Division II team that included my teammate Dallas Thornton. We traveled with four Division I teams, one Army team, and played in several different spots around the United States. We wound up in Albuquerque, New Mexico, where the championships were played and selections for the Olympic team were made.

As the lead scorer in my division, I felt I had a good opportunity to make the team. But I sprained my ankle prior to the final games and was not able to play through the end of the competition. I did not make the 1968 Olympic team, but I was approached to stay ready just in case someone was hurt. No Division II player had ever made the US Olympic Team.

The assassination of Martin Luther King, Jr. occurred right in the middle of the trials and marred the event for a lot of us. When the news hit, several players went out into the halls of our hotel and started destroying things. Others just stayed in their rooms. The killing of our national leader also hit me like a blow to the middle of my heart. But, as was my nature, I carried the pain internally rather than openly display my emotions.

I had been raised by Mama. It was just her and I. Once she passed it was up to me to take care of me. Emotionally I was distraught with what was happening in our nation. During the Olympic tryouts, a lot of key basketball athletes like Kareem Abdul-Jabbar, Elvin Hayes, and Wes Unseld chose not to participate in the overall tryouts.

Other sports were affected also. My perspective of the Black Power movement was based on my experiences growing up at Green Street Baptist Church, the community leaders there, and surrounding Smoketown. Martin Luther King's nonviolence approach was my method of choice as I dealt with the realities before me. I had a mission that I felt Mama wanted me to achieve and Christian beliefs as I understood them.

Having attended majority-white educational institutions since desegregation, I had not learned a great deal about our Black history other than what was taught at home, church, and in our community. The schools I attended only briefly touched upon Black history. This might have had something to do with the fact that all my teachers and coaches were white from fifth grade through college.

A NONVIOLENT APPROACH

I made a conscious decision to pursue the nonviolent approach to make a positive impact on my community and be more productive. I strove to do my best while giving back to those who were less fortunate. Additionally, I had a strong desire to learn more about my Black family history, as it gave me a wider perspective. I knew I was in an underdog position in life, but through athletics, I could reach a platform to be an effective leader while motivating others to do the same.

Our basketball team at KWC was made up of a small minority of Black players who stuck together. We had several white players, in particular Dick O'Neill from New York, who had no problem being very comfortable around our small group in our freshman year. For other teammates, it took longer for them to come together off the court of play. The trip to Africa certainly brought our entire team of white and Black players closer together even though we had mixed opinions of what we experienced.

One instance in particular was transformative when we visited Dahomey. This was where the slave ships departed en route to the United States and other islands along the way. We learned how from the African standpoint, slave trade was a cultural thing that had been going on for centuries.

The entire late 1960s and early 1970s was the beginning of the revolutionary movement. We all chose our course of action and my path was a nonviolent but aggressive approach toward making a positive impact on my community as a leader. As a Black athlete, our choices were limited in getting a college scholarship and we had to pave a way to open doors for more Black opportunities along with getting an education.

COLLEGE LIFE

In my college experience and beyond, I received every Hall of Fame honor that Kentucky Wesleyan has to offer. I am honored to have been fortunate enough to receive them. I am proud that I was able to exemplify each honor including the Honorary Doctorate Degree as a Humanitarian. I am not one to brag, but I would compare my experience as a college student-athlete with anyone's.

Kentucky Wesleyan has honored me twice as the number one basketball player of all time. My career on and off the court can be matched by none, both statistically and in academic achievement over four years. I was voted to the All-Century Team in the NCAA D-II, Kentucky Athletic Hall of Fame, Small College Hall of Fame, KWC Alumni Hall of Fame, KWC Athletic Hall of Fame, and gave the 2009 Commencement Speech as the first athlete and first Black to do so.

I was also Sigma Alpha Mu Fraternity Athlete of the Year—the fraternity of David Stern, commissioner of the NBA, and football Hall of Famers Jim Brown and Ernie Davis. I thank my coaches, Guy Strong and Bob Daniels, for their guidance. I also want to thank Nurse Lucy Fullerton and Dr. Robert Cockrum, my professor, and all of my teammates for making these awards possible. Lastly, I want to thank my wife whom I met and started dating at KWC.

My goal in college was to be the very best I could be both on and off the court while contributing to my team and college success. I was always excited to take the trophies home and show my sister Mary, Clarence, Olivia, and some neighbors what I had accomplished.

Once I achieved one award, I was only that much more motivated to achieve more.

Of all the unexpected windfalls of that era, the trip to Europe and Africa was one of the biggest. And to think, it almost didn't happen due to a last-minute snag. When the team started planning the trip, I encountered a problem. I had been known my entire life as George Tinsley. I was even enrolled as George Tinsley at KWC. The NCAA listed me as George Tinsley when the trip was arranged.

However, my draft card was the only official document I had to prove my identification, and it identified me as George Wm. Penebaker Tinsley. Thus, I needed to obtain a passport in the name of George Tinsley, but when the coaches applied for our passports, my passport came back George William Penebaker rather than George Tinsley. That was when the confusion started. We were finally able to get me a passport that everyone agreed upon, which was George William Penebaker.

Mrs. Lucy Fullerton, the college nurse, came to the rescue and agreed to assist me with the change once I returned from the trip abroad. Mrs. Fullerton had already taken a strong interest in me early in my freshman year. She helped with the paperwork to have my name officially declared as George Tinsley.

Still a teenager not long out of Smoketown, I had never even imagined flying. But there I was, in a huge jetliner, surrounded by teammates, off on a grand tour across the Atlantic. It was exhilarating and scary all at once. We spent half of that summer traveling from one country to another.

We flew first from New York City to London. After a whirlwind daylong tour there, we carried on to Morocco, Chad, Cameroon, Togo, Niger, Senegal, and eventually back to New York and home to Louisville. At each stop, we played an exhibition game. Our format was typically training sessions in the morning, playing an exhibition game early afternoon, and attending receptions hosted by diplomats and high-level local officials at night. Of course, when we could, we went sightseeing. Staying in better-than-average hotels and eating in comfortable restaurants was a new world for me and the other players. On the trip were two coaches, one referee, and ten players, of which three were Black.

When we first arrived in Chad, it was late evening. We checked into our hotel rooms. Joe and I were staying in one room while Dallas Thornton and Dick One roomed in another. Dick was white, and this meant it was the first time a white and Black player roomed together. All the players came to my room to look out on the balcony as the Africans were beginning to go to work while singing and chanting rhythms. One of the white players asked me what they were singing, and I jokingly said, "They are coming to get you in the morning," so get some rest! That started the trip off with lots of relaxing humor.

One of the other positive aspects of my years at KWC was the popularity I gained in the KWC community. Beginning as early as my freshman year I started developing strong relationships with the student body and the professors. Unlike most of my teammates, I didn't leave campus and go into town regularly; I was more comfortable staying on campus. That allowed me to meet and become friends with students from all over the country.

As I progressed into my sophomore and junior years, my campus status rose to the next level. Much of that resulted from being a starter on the NCAA championship team; I was more accessible, reachable, and had a reputation of having a friendly personality. In my sophomore year we had probably the best team we'd ever had. We didn't win the championship that year, but we did go to the semifinals and came in third place. I became ill and was hospitalized during the finals and was unable to play the last two games. I always teased my teammates that we lost because I was not there.

As a result of all the attention, my self-esteem was also bounding like crazy. After years of being the guy who shied away from social engagement, being one of the centers of attention was a new world for me. This phase peaked toward the end of my senior year on what was known as Senior Day for the basketball team. During halftime at our Senior Day game, all the senior athletes would come out on the court with their parents as we were announced to the crowd.

Clarence and Olivia, who were there as my guardians, came and stood with me. This was the first time that the two of them had ever attended a basketball game and seen me play high school or college. They were dressed to the nines and bursting with excitement. Given that my last name was Tinsley, we were a focal point of the ceremony and the last to be introduced.

During that event, I took a minute to reflect on how far I had come. Although I had graduated from Male High in good standing, I had no preparation for college. I never really looked at taking any of the extra steps that other students did to prepare for college, such as buying more adult clothing and dorm decor. Instead, I arrived at college in a two-seater Corvette, wedged between two of my high school teammates Dallas Thornton and Van Stinnett, with nothing but a little bag of my belongings in my lap. Van came from a wealthy family. His dad was a doctor, and Van drove a different car every day during high school. He was a good friend, and even though he was a white player, he blended in well with his Black teammates.

OFF-THE-COURT CHALLENGES

But as natural as being on the court felt, that was just about the only part of college that felt natural. My early academic performance was dismal, to the point I almost got removed from the team—something I couldn't help but reflect on that Senior Day. I had a 2.5 GPA in the first semester of my freshman year. Once basketball season started, it fell to 1.75. By the end of that first year, I was on academic probation. After the whirlwind summer trip to Europe and Africa, I returned to school to do a lot of makeup work to come off academic probation by the time the basketball season started. The possibility of losing my scholarship and getting kicked off the team was a scary period.

Like many first-year students, I had lousy study habits. I had mimicked what some other upper-class athletes were doing, choosing a poor schedule of early morning classes and missing way too many. I struggled to get up to attend a Music Appreciation or Old Testament Bible class at 8:00 a.m. I was not disciplined, and I was convinced by others that because I played basketball, I would pass the classes.

How could I turn this obstacle into an opportunity? As usual, my first instinct was to reach into my inner resources. Once I put my mind to it, I knew how to get schoolwork done. I started going to summer school. For two years in a row, rather than return to Louisville, I stayed in Owensboro, worked, and went to school. I discovered that I could take some tougher courses during the summer and get higher grades, making my share of As and Bs.

I also turned to Joel Bolden, the friend I had known since fifth grade who was now a college classmate. Joe was a better student than I was. He had gone to a Catholic school, and this prepared him for college. We were very good friends and were determined, come hell or high water, to push through until we had our college diplomas in hand.

There were fraternities and sororities on campus for students to join if accepted by that fraternity. But there was no Black fraternity on campus, and the fraternities that were on campus did not admit Blacks, with the exception of one. I was recruited and joined the Sigma Alpha Mu Fraternity; this was a Jewish fraternity on campus, which, in my junior year, had just become a chapter graduation from a colony.

I'd become friends with a few of the members, and they were mostly from the northeast. The fraternity had notable members on other campuses who were Black, including Black athletes like Jim Brown and Ernie Davis, both of Syracuse University. This was a smart move, and it made me part of a circle of guys who were very focused on classroom learning and academic achievement along with the community. They were good students and offered me peer guidance and counseling. I had a group of guys that I studied with and who were outstanding students. They kept files of the various testing methods used by different professors. As we studied, we could draw from those documents. That gave me access to many tools and resources I didn't have before.

By leaning into academic work, turning for help to professors and some of my peers, and just studying harder, I was able to turn my unimpressive freshman-year classroom performance around. By junior and senior year, I was doing well in academic work as well as sports. The summer classes did not hurt either.

DEVELOPING A SUPPORT NETWORK

Just as in junior high and high school, I developed a small circle of supporters who were mentors and substitute family members. Nurse Fullerton, who assisted me in getting my passport for the trip abroad to Europe and Africa, remained a supporter and mother figure throughout my college years. In my sophomore year, I broke my nose in practice. She came to the practice site, went to the hospital with me, and remained until I got that fixed. Later on that same year, I came down with mononucleosis, and they put me in the hospital. She helped see me through that, too.

Coach Strong, who offered me a scholarship also gave me tough-love support and pushed me to be the best I could be. He'd taken notice of me as a young teenager and recruited me to Male High but left to take the job at KWC. He also recruited Joel Bolden and Van Stinnett from Louisville. Van was a teammate of mine at Male. We had six freshmen come into KWC together, Tommy Hobgood, Dick O'Neill, Stephen Deskins, Van Stinnett, Joel Bolden, and myself.

We were the first class to attend all four years and graduate together. The other teammates, like Sam Smith, Dallas Thornton, Roger Cordell, Don Bradley, John Chapman, Jesse Flynn, and Ernie Simpson, were already there and were the nucleus of a very good team. Coach Strong and Coach Bob Daniels had recruited a strong team of young players. Over the next four years, five more former players from Louisville would form the core of the Panthers. We were unique during the mid-1960s in that Coach Strong was not afraid to start three Black players during those tough years.

A young woman named Seretha Summers undoubtedly had the most significant impact on my college life. Also from Louisville, she came to KWC as a freshman and was the only African American woman on campus. We knew one another casually from high school. I had been a senior while she was a sophomore there at Male High School. Now I recognized that she was everything: a beauty, academically strong, well-liked, and very caring. My teammate Dallas Thornton knew her very well and much longer than I did. They had mutual friends, and he knew her parents well.

Seretha lived in the women's dorm. All her dorm mates seemed crazy about her from the time she arrived. She shined in that kind of setting. She liked to step out and take on challenges. As the chaplain of her first-year class, she also prayed with her classmates who had problems. In all, she was a bright light on campus. In particular, the several young women from rural areas of Kentucky, who had in many cases never been around Black people, were just blown away by her.

During my junior year, the school held a Sadie Hawkins Dance, an annual event where the girls had to chase the guys, catch them, and put a tag on them. The guy who was tagged had to go to the dance with the young lady. I think the girls talked her into chasing me. Of course, I didn't run too hard, and she caught me!

Seretha and I went to the dance together, and that's where it all started. From there, our relationship grew stronger every year. And it has for the past five decades.

I credit many of my successes in that period with the dialogues that she and I were having about success and doing the right thing. She made it clear that she wanted to see me be successful in a caring, supportive way. Coming from a successful family, she also wanted to be successful in the things she was doing.

Besides the supportive conversations, Seretha and I were named king and queen of the campus in one of the school functions during my senior and her sophomore year. In my senior year, we became a focal point for the campus and local media. The campus media started photographing us at different marketing events, and we ended up on the covers of several athletic programs, among other school publications. I think the media liked the idea of doing stories on Seretha and myself as a couple, along with me being the star of the basketball team. We were thrown out there as a kind of model couple. And that set the tone for the life we would share for decades.

Graduation was, of course, a milestone. I became the first in my family to receive a college diploma. I was also one of the first Black athletes to graduate from KWC, alongside my friend Joel Bolden. We were possibly the first Blacks to live on campus and graduate in the school's long history. Others had come but, for one reason or another, had not received their diplomas during their four years on scholarship up until that point. Joel and I were the first. I was honored to share that achievement with him. In reaching that milestone, Joel and I set an example. In later years many other Black athletes would get KWC diplomas.

As my time at Kentucky Wesleyan started to wind down, I started to focus on what lay ahead for me postcollege. I had entered Kentucky Wesleyan with a career in teaching in mind; playing professional basketball was a faint pipe dream. But as my game improved, that scenario changed before my eyes. Two of my teammates, Sam Smith and Dallas Thornton, had gone on to play professional basketball. My career achievements were statistically equal to or better than theirs, so therefore I felt I had a very good opportunity to get drafted into both the National Basketball Association and the American Basketball Association.

During my senior year, an agent approached me. That was the standard way for players to communicate with professional teams and determine which teams looked at them as possible draft choices.

The catch was that I couldn't sign with an agent while I was playing in college, or I would become ineligible to play the remainder of my college career. I had to wait until my senior basketball season had concluded.

Still, throughout the season, several scouts from the ABA and NBA came to the games to watch us play. I had no contact or conversations with them, but I recognized at least one. My old high school coach, who had become coach of the American Basketball Association Kentucky Colonels, attended several games. Of course, many others came. When I realized there were many eyes on me on the court, and knowing my old coach was there, I understood that a professional basketball career was no longer a pipe dream. It was right there within my reach.

CHAPTER FOUR

PRO BASKETBALL

Getting drafted by a professional basketball team marked the beginning of new possibilities in life for me. The highlight came a few months after the American Basketball Association Oakland Oaks first drafted me. They had just won the ABA Championship and had several all-ABA players on that team, along with Rick Barry, Larry Brown, and Warren Jabali, who are now Hall of Fame players.

My contract was soon to be bought by the Kentucky Colonels and stepping onto the court as a player on my hometown team was even a greater dream come true. In the best moments of that phase, all of the athletic skills, successes at Smoketown's Ballard Park, Louisville's Dirt Bowl summer competition, and in the Louisville Male High basketball program and in Kentucky Wesleyan's four straight NCAA finals and three NCAA championships seemed to come together in a perfect storm, with an opportunity to be successful in the game that I love while getting paid for my performance.

I signed with the Oakland Oaks, but prior to training camp the team folded, and the team's Washington, DC, ownership decided to bring the team to DC. So I moved to DC, started training camp there, and after playing five games with the newly minted Washington Caps my contract was purchased by the Kentucky Colonels. My first game with them was in New York against the New York Nets, but being on the Kentucky Colonels meant I was back to primarily playing in my home city again. During the season, one of the finest events of my newfound status as a professional basketball player came halfway into my first season with the Colonels in a face-off against the Los Angeles Stars.

I was typically the first substitute at small forward or the second substitute as a big guard during the season. The coach inserted me as a small forward to guard Willie Wise, a six-five All-Star small forward for the Stars. Checking the star players on the other teams was a main factor in the Colonels' decision to purchase my contract from the Caps. But this time, as we transitioned back and forth from offense to defense, I had the opening to showcase my offensive skills, particularly my scoring ability. And boy, did I take advantage of the opportunity, becoming the second leading scorer in that particular game and only missing one shot attempt.

My approach was to always "fill the lanes"—an old basketball term, describing the fundamental practice of getting a defensive rebound so your team can turn the rebound into an organized fast break. Depending on where you are on the court, you would make sure that all "lanes" were filled moving down toward your offensive opportunity to score. I was very good at filling the lanes, regardless of whether I had the ball or the point guards had the ball. That night, my shot was clicking. It seemed like everything I put up there was going in. I hit seven shots in a row and had scored eighteen points going into the fourth quarter.

During a timeout, the trainer approached me, beaming with excitement. "You hit seven shots in a row," he said. "You haven't missed one." As seemed to always be the case, those comments broke my string of not missing a shot attempt. My streak came to a close.

In my three-year career with the American Basketball Association, I played a few games like that, hitting on all cylinders, holding my own as a defensive player, and racking up some significant points. My forte really was as a defensive player, offensive player, and team player. But playing professionally in the ABA was a business, where putting butts in seats was the key to success. Having attended a small D-II institution was not a drawing card, when you were up against the major institution player who had large followings. All teams in the ABA had tremendous problems making a profit and would fold either during or after the season ended. Every team that I played on folded, with the exception of the Colonels, who always maintained players from local major college programs on the roster.

Therefore if you were not a special talented player or a Division I high-profile player, you had to take a back seat to the stars of the particular team. With Kentucky, I had a deft pick-and-roll going with our centers Gene Moore and Bud Olsen. And I made sure I got open for shots if my teammates ever decided to pass to the center position on certain play actions. I had the fundamentals of the game down pat. I might not have been the most outstanding player, but I could hold my own. The combination of defensive skills and knowledge of the fundamentals kept me in play during that period. That game against the LA Stars was probably the one occasion where I had the opportunity to display my offensive skill set during the game in front of the home crowd. I always knew that I was a very good player, but I knew that I had to wait my turn to show how good I was during a game. I finished the season with the Colonels averaging eight points a game with limited playing time and focusing on defense. These days it would be called a role player who understood his assignment.

Getting to that spot where I felt totally confident as a professional ball player was a long, winding, and often challenging process. As always, opportunities came, and so did obstacles. Having been a star player in college and having confidence in my skills, it was difficult to be patient.

MY FIRST SEASON

I started the journey during my first season when I was fresh out of college. NBA and ABA scouts were eyeing me, and I occasionally saw them in the stands. I had an excellent career as a college player. I had come from an environment where I was a key player, a two-time All-American during my four years, as I pondered the possibilities of getting drafted, the pros and cons of the National Basketball Association versus the American Basketball Association and the various teams in each league. The Chicago Bulls team seemed to be a good fit for me.

The Bulls had a reputation as a hard-nosed, defensive team. They were looking at me, and I was hopeful they would pick me. In the end, both the Bulls and the Oakland Oaks drafted me. The difference was that Oakland drafted me in the second round, and the Bulls drafted me in the sixth round; the Oaks offered a $25,000 contract with a $10,000 signing bonus.

The Bulls, I had to attend the tryout camps with no signing bonus. I opted for Oakland and was excited to have the opportunity to make the team and join them and wide open to what the experience of playing with a professional team would bring. But then, right out of the starting gates came the first of what would be several unexpected turns in my professional basketball journey. Before I could join the Oaks, the Washington Capitals—the Washington, DC, area team—bought the Oaks.

Instead of going west, I headed north to the nation's capital to start training. I was brimming with anticipation and excitement. During the drive in my new 1969 GTO, I pondered what it would be like to join the Caps, which had just won the ABA championship as the Oakland Oaks. It was a great team, made all the better by some All-Star players: Rick Barry, a forward; Larry Brown, a point guard; and Warren Jabali, a multitalented guard/forward. With that kind of star power, joining the starting lineup would be tough. But I felt I could fit in and play.

I arrived about two weeks before training camp started and began working out. When training camp started you could wear any jersey, so I started practice wearing Rick Barry's number 24—since he was arriving late and the team was not sure if he was even coming to DC. Larry Brown and I hit it off from the start. He mentored me and offered a lot of insights as we practiced. He had come over from the Oaks, where he had built a reputation as a player-coach on the floor. I listened closely to the lessons he shared.

When the season started, I was put in the rotation. I was the first forward to go in the games. But then, five games into the season, I arrived at another of those unexpected turns in my journey as a rookie pro player. One afternoon after practice, I entered the locker room and found that my name had been pulled off my locker. I was scared that I had been abruptly cut, but then the trainer explained that the Kentucky Colonels had bought my contract. He handed me a plane ticket and told me that I was scheduled to meet with my new team in New York City the next day.

I was thrilled to be joining the Colonels but devastated by how this all went down with the communications from the front office. I was excited because this meant going back to my hometown of Louisville! It was a comfort zone for me, with family, friends, and a fan base there. Perhaps more importantly, Seretha was there, too, and our relationship was growing closer than ever. I also knew most of the players on the team, including starting forward Sam Smith, my former college teammate for two years at Kentucky Wesleyan College where we won an NCAA championship together.

Even before I started playing with the Colonels, I understood why they had picked me. For one, I was a well-known and much-appreciated player in the Louisville area, where they were based. But, more importantly, the Colonels needed to bolster their defense. Among their rivals were teams such as the Indiana Pacers. They had an ABA All-Star small-forward player who was six-foot-five and an excellent scorer. The Colonels needed to have a reliable player who could defend these All-Stars. And as I said, defense was my forte, and my former high school coach and now the head coach of the Colonels knew that.

Still, I had some worries. One was Gene Rhodes, the Colonels' head coach. He had been my coach at Male High School. We didn't always see eye to eye in those years, and I foresaw some complications, given that he knew me as a defensive player and a rebounder, not a scorer. Soon after joining the Colonels squad, I saw that some of my concerns were justified. Clearly, being a standout on the team would take more than having skills on the court.

The biggest issue was that the plays were designed to get the ball to guards who were the star players—the marquee names on the team. When I joined, there were two stars: Darrell Carrier and Louie Dampier. Both were guards and were the central focus of the team's offense. They could light it up. One averaged twenty-five points per game, and the other about twenty-three points. They were probably two of the greatest three-point shooters in ABA history. Darrell was a little less likely to get his shot off the dribble and needed a pick to get open. Louie could get his shot off and handle the ball exceptionally well. The setups were all geared to getting the two of them open so they could do what they did best.

The coaches and owners wanted the two of them to rack up points. Their star power would bring in the crowds. And bigger audiences would translate into more significant ticket sales and thus higher revenues.

While that arrangement worked well for the owners and coaches, it left me—and other players—in a dilemma. I was confident that I could score. Given the right circumstances, I could even be a high scorer. When I did get a chance to get in the game, every sign suggested that I could be more of a contributor. And the fans loved me.

"We want Tinsley," came the cries from the bleachers. "We want Tinsley."

Of course, many of my teammates had their fans as well. This was my hometown, Louisville, Kentucky. After all, my friends and family were cheering for me, given my hometown's reputation. The Louisville crowd always turned up when we played at the Louisville Convention Center, which was only a few miles from where I grew up, and they were always raucous.

And yet, the basic plays were not designed for me or other forwards to score as the first option. It was a plus for me—or any other player on the team who was not a designated shooter—to score twenty-plus points. Given the particular personal contracts, there was a problem if the stars did not meet their contractual goals to receive the bonuses they were counting on.

Even when I was on a roll, scoring points right and left, Coach Rhodes and ownership did not fully embrace the moment. As soon as I missed a shot, they would take me out of the game and put me back on the bench. They fell back into prioritizing getting the guys on the court who scored points and brought fans to the games.

That memorable game against the Los Angeles Stars, when I was hitting every shot I took, is an excellent example of how even the best of my times as a professional player ended on down notes. I had all cylinders clicking, hitting everything I threw up. The whole place was abuzz, with my fans cheering and me feeling in my prime. But then I missed one shot (only after, I'll remind you, I'd just made seven shots in a row), and the coach sent me back to the bench.

This syndrome of coaches and owners favoring the stars was not only true of the Colonels. It was prevalent throughout the league in particular terms that were not financially strong. At that time, I didn't fully understand the business of the ABA and what was going on behind the scenes. But I knew what I saw—perfectly competent players were there one day and gone the next. Constant cutting and trading were part of the system. To keep their businesses going, owners and coaches were always looking for new angles to get fans in the arenas. Winning was important, but getting butts in seats was the priority in order to pay the overhead.

THE CHALLENGES

Besides the revolving door of players, other issues came up. While I was ultimately in the game for the love of the sport, money was also an issue. Professional basketball players were not getting anywhere near what they make today. For the starting players, the average salary was in the $30,000 to $40,000 range. A star like Julius Erving made $125,000 a year in 1971. The pay was far less for the players who were not starters but part of the rotation, like me. Most players signed a one-year contract, which had to be renegotiated each year; their salaries typically dropped if not a starter. I was caught up in that cycle. In my second year, I made $15,000 a year, which was probably the average salary for most of the guys coming off the bench. Some guys were even paid by the game with incentives for rebounds, defensive assignments, or performing duties for the team off the court.

The traveling and living conditions were also far from ideal on the road. Players typically made the best of travel by cars or regular passenger planes. We typically worked during the off-season to be able to purchase homes. Our positions and futures were not guaranteed, so entering a long-term payment arrangement on a house didn't always make sense. We never knew from game to game or one year to the next where we would be or what our status might be.

Competition between teammates was tough, too, even at times cutthroat. You had to be careful about what you shared with others on the team. Some would take any negative information back to the coach or the team. On top of that, some of the players were into heavy drug use. To be clear, there were good clean guys on the team—stable, married, and worthy role models. But at the same time, there was drug use, which was impossible to ignore. We also had guys who had been incarcerated in the league and had just gotten out of prison. They had issues that needed counseling, but it was not available through the league at the time.

I learned to deal with the insecurities of being in an unstable situation and everything that came with that. Despite the challenges, I remained committed to the game and gave it my best. By that stage, I was in my mid-twenties and had learned not to be daunted by adversity. In a league that lacked stability, where players were constantly coming and going, Kentucky was probably as stable as any team in the league. We at least weren't worried about our checks bouncing like some players on other teams.

I did well during the training camps in my second season with the Colonels, or so I thought. My game had improved. I was averaging twenty-plus points in my practice games. But then, just as I thought I had found solid footing as a professional player came another unexpected turn in my journey. The Colonels had drafted several guys from the University of Kentucky along with other local colleges—Artis Gilmore, Dan Issel, Mike Pratt, Claude Virden, to name a few. There was a new general manager, Mike Storen, and an ownership status change with some financial difficulties.

Despite my achievements and the improvements in my game, the Colonels released me midway through the year. That decision came unexpectedly and dealt me a hard blow. *What would I do now?* But as always, I faced the obstacle and tried to turn it into something positive and productive. The one constant was that I had a college degree and knew that I could always fall back on it.

I wound up joining the Miami Floridians the next year. It was not as strong a squad as the Colonels, but there were some excellent opportunities for me to play. As always, there were some complications with a new team, new players, and coaches. The head coach, Bob Bass, had some close relationships with some of the players he'd known since college, and he favored them. There were also two guards, Larry Jones and Mack Calvin, two All-Star players, one who had come from the Los Angeles Stars team. There was also Warren Jabali, who was an All-Star, all of whom were averaging twenty points or more. That meant there were fewer opportunities to score, so defense was the focus opportunity here. That, in turn, translated into fewer opportunities for me at the start of the season.

As long as I was on the team and getting some time on the court, I felt confident I was developing. But in Miami, the coach rotated me in less and less. If I was lucky, I might have played three games in a row and had an essential part of those games. But then, I might not play at all for the next three games. Not having time on the court was probably the worst thing to happen to me and my mental state of mind. I didn't handle it well psychologically. I let my anger and other emotions out verbally or physically in practice and on the court.

My year with Miami was one of the most challenging stretches of my pro career. Thoughts started swirling about whether I was on the right team and if my career was ending soon. Those thoughts often took me back to my college years. It had seemed like a perfect utopian situation. I had succeeded on the court and in the classroom.

Along the way, I learned what success felt like, and I relished that feeling. Following my last year in high school, I had not really experienced failure or been seen as a failure. In my mind and soul, I could achieve just about any objective I set my mind to. And the course of events proved my point. Getting into college, winning three national championships, and then having the opportunity to participate in the 1968 Olympics helped to build up my path of success and my spirit of winning. I went into professional basketball with star status on my mind. I was quickly hit with the harsh reality that I could not be as successful or as experienced as I thought I could be. On the contrary, I was beginning to feel like I was a failure in the league.

Fortunately, some new developments in my life distracted me from hard knocks happening with the league. By far, the most significant event was the decision to get engaged to Seretha with intentions to marry the love of my life. Our union seemed inevitable in my mind from the day when we met, and now we were forging ahead with plans to make it official. I also had some exciting leads about who and where my birth family might be, which I'll talk more about in chapter 5, and I began to research the trail.

Still, that sense of failure hung over me for a long time. Navigating through it was one of the most brutal struggles I have ever dealt with. When I wasn't playing games or practicing, I was at home mulling things over. That process went on for a while. And then, finally, I made one of the most significant decisions of my life. It was time to stop struggling in the ABA or traveling overseas to play. I had a degree and had to move on with a new profession.

The decision to leave professional basketball was significant. It wasn't my plan. But it was God's plan. Once I had made the decision, I could transfer my desire for success into everything else I was doing. Once again, I learned to overcome an obstacle and turn it into an opportunity. I was still very interested in playing, but I followed my priorities and pursued things I had to do in my life.

I could always pursue my passion for basketball in other ways than being a professional player. I could still walk on local teams. One event that I got engaged in was the Louisville Dirt Bowl, which was a summer basketball tradition. It was an annual tournament held in Louisville, where all the former professionals in the area, including many who had been in the NBA and the ABA, came back and played in the summer. The games were played in Shawnee Park. My squad for the Dirt Bowl won the pro division seven years in a row. In terms of popular appeal, the team was probably on the same level as the Kentucky Colonels. The games were played on Sunday afternoons and evenings, and basketball fans from all over the city came early to get seating and enjoy the games. It would take fans hours just to drive into the park and get to the courts. Engagement with the Dirt Bowl allowed me and other players the chance to enjoy the game that we love and entertain our fans.

CHAPTER FIVE

A NEW FAMILY
AND NEW LIFE

When I reflect on the major milestones of my life—the passing of Mama, my graduation from Male High School, the scholarship to Kentucky Wesleyan College, three NCAA championships, graduating from college with a degree and awards, and so on—1972 turned out to have been one of the most consequential years of my life. Starting in the spring of my twenty-fifth year, I experienced several events that were life changing. Together, the experiences impacted everything, from my sense of identity to my life's mission. My emotional state was rocked to the bone with life-changing decisions.

The highlight of my entire life occurred in April 1972 with my marriage to Seretha. A few weeks later, on a May afternoon in Louisville, the two of us were hanging out in the basement of my new in-laws' home. Everything seemed normal, but what we didn't know then was that we were only moments away from embarking on what would prove to be a long roller-coaster ride and an emotional year.

"George," my mother-in-law called out from upstairs. "Can you come up? There's someone here I want you to meet."

I thought it might be a neighbor or acquaintance. In that era, when I was a professional basketball player, I had gotten used to fans approaching me to chat. As I went to join her, I anticipated a quick meet-and-greet encounter.

At the top of the stairs, a man was standing in the door. I didn't know who he was, but as we stared one another in the eye, I felt a flash of familiarity come over me.

"George, I want you to meet June Penebaker," my mother-in-law said. When those words came out, I can't even describe the rush of feelings that went through me. It was fantastic in a real sense, but there was a little sense of anger.

Then my mother-in-law turned to the man and said, "This is your son, George Penebaker Tinsley."

"Well, I didn't know anything about you," I remember him saying. "If I'd known, I would have come and got you as a child, as I did with your older brother."

And just like that, what had started out as another Saturday at my in-laws' became one of the most consequential days of my life.

Since adolescence, I'd known that even though Mama had raised me, she and her family were not my blood kin. I was raised knowing that my birth mother had left me at Mama's when I was a baby. I knew nothing about my father except his name, which appeared on my birth certificate. Getting engaged sparked a new interest in discovering the missing part of my life: my birth family. With Seretha's urging, I started to put threads together to try to find them. I asked my sister, Mary, many deep and probing questions during this time, hoping to learn as much information as possible that would maybe give me a lead to follow. She loved and understood me and would reluctantly give me bits of information. Clarence, on the other hand, would not understand the question, given that he had a deep dislike for my mother and their past relationship.

At the same time, my in-laws started to get involved. They knew both my mother's and father's families, as they all were raised in the same part of Louisville, called the "Bottoms." My mother-in-law and my father had grown up in the same area of the city. Her brother had known my father and played baseball with him. When they heard he was in town for the Kentucky Derby they decided to invite him over to visit.

In that first encounter, my father came across as a very straightforward and somewhat aggressive guy. Although my character is much different, I could see and feel a strange connection. For a son to meet his father this way was naturally quite awkward, to say the least. We didn't look much alike, but many things about him resonated with me.

That unexpected father/son meeting was my introduction to my birth family, and the start of a union of sixteen brothers and sisters, plus a whole network of aunts, uncles, and cousins to come.

For all the drama of that afternoon and the follow-up uniting with family, that was far from the most significant life passage that would occur in 1972. This was also the year that I decided to leave professional basketball after being released from the New York Nets. I had to decide whether to report to Dallas, Texas, for further tryouts with the Dallas Chaparrals or to settle back at home for a different career opportunity.

I will discuss this in more detail later, but my choice to pivot my career came after a long period of soul-searching. I felt that I had lost a lot of my professional basketball training focus due to finding this new family and traveling to meet everyone. Not to mention the fact that I had recently gotten married.

SERETHA

Let me offer some background that might help clarify the significance of our union. By the time Seretha and I exchanged vows, we had already known one another for several years, having met in high school. Even back then, when I first caught a glimpse of her in the halls of Male High, it was love at first sight. She had a boyfriend at that time, a classmate of mine, so I kept my distance out of respect. I, quite frankly, did not feel that I could live up to her standards due to my personal situation and lack of self-esteem, so I kept my head down and went off to college.

But then in 1968, in my junior year at Kentucky Wesleyan, Seretha joined me there, enrolling as a freshman. She was the only African American girl on campus, and I was a star on the basketball team that was ranked number one in the nation. We just had a natural pull toward each other which was encouraged by fellow classmates and professors.

We shared our first dance and kiss at the Sadie Hawkins Dance. Despite her having a boyfriend at the time, it wasn't long before they broke up and we started dating. Our appreciation of one another only grew stronger as the year passed along.

Somewhere in the middle of that period of dating, I wrote a letter to Seretha. In it, I talked about how much we had in common and how our life goals and plans were similar. If we ever got together and got married, I wrote, I believed that we could be successful in all the areas we discussed.

The letter was in keeping with the dynamic that had developed between us. Even back then, she was always encouraging with my education and athletic goals. One of the critical ways she expressed her deep feelings for me was to challenge me constantly to be the best

I could be. She attended and became a part of our basketball games. She was a pacesetter (dance team) and later became a cheerleader. She also set her sights on being successful in her own right, and I always stood by her as she pursued her goals. We supported one another.

It should be no surprise that in the year Seretha and I started dating, things began to turn around in my life. I'd always wanted to make her happy, and for her to see me as a success. As a result, I stayed focused on my goals, and positive events started happening, many of which I attribute to the conversation Seretha and I shared about success and doing the right thing.

Not only did I become a two-time All-American during my junior and senior years, but my GPA took a turn for the better. I started making the Dean's List and was thriving as a person. I loved Seretha, and I was motivated by who I was when I was with her. Years after I wrote that letter, graduated from KWC, and was playing professional basketball, our wedding came and sealed the romance between us that had been blossoming for years. Married now to the woman of my dreams, a woman who was and is beautiful to me in every way, gave me a kind of completeness that I had never known.

Our wedding ceremony, which took place on April 29, 1972, was unique. Seretha's mother and stepfather were very well-known in the community, and her biological father was an iconic figure who owned a local radio station. He was also a minister. Everything about the wedding had to be just right, and so her family ensured that things were done appropriately, and Seretha was also a big part of the planning process.

We were married in Seretha's father's church. Her biological dad married us, and her stepfather gave her away. My nephew, Mary's son, who was like a younger brother to me, was my best man. It was a very happy occasion, marking the culmination of a four-year romance and the beginning of our new lives together.

For me, it was also a new start in a life that I wanted to spend with my best friend and love. We had spent several years talking about and planning our next life after giving back to those who helped us through life to that point, and our union solidified the partnership of setting and reaching goals we had started in our dating years.

In marriage, more than ever, Seretha gave me the confidence and drive to be ambitious. Of course, I have done the same for her. I encouraged her career in everything that she has gone after, from being an elementary school teacher to a radio station executive in cities such as Louisville, Atlanta, and Jacksonville to her civic pursuits in Central Florida. She will always say that she gave up her career in radio to help me pursue my dreams, and I cannot express how thankful I am and how much I appreciate her for doing so.

With my marriage to Seretha, I also became part of her family. I must say that her mother became my closest ally from the day we first met. I found a lot of happiness with her family. My mother-in-law always stayed connected with us and with me in particular. She and I had a powerful relationship. She helped quite a bit when troubles arose, and I probably talked with her about things more than anybody else because she was a social worker by profession. She was an excellent listener who didn't take sides. She looked and listened to the big picture and gave me constructive feedback.

Of my two new fathers-in-law, Seretha's stepfather was a wonderful businessman and consultant in the Louisville community, and he was very supportive of my career but with caution, given my limited background in business. Seretha's birth father, an entrepreneur in his own right, was the last person I asked about marrying his daughter, and as it turned out, he was the easiest person to talk to and gave me some straightforward advice. He gave me some pretty good information that has lasted throughout my fifty-two years with his daughter. These conversations also helped clarify that my decisions, particularly regarding my career, were not only about my wishes. I had to think about meeting the demands of a family.

Looking back over more than five decades of marriage, Seretha and I have accomplished just about all the goals and more that we discussed early in our dating. We've had successful business careers, raised a family, and saved enough that we don't have financial worries.

The one exception would be more children. We wanted to have more children. Back then, we talked about raising ten or twelve children. Once we started being parents, difficulties emerged that precluded us from achieving that earlier goal. Beyond that, Seretha was a success-motivated person who wanted to accomplish things. Having many more children wouldn't have allowed her or us to grow as much in our profession. In the end, Penni and George II were just the right fit.

FINDING STABILITY

I had left college on a high note. My successes on the basketball courts and in the classroom left me with a drive to reach for the stars. I thought whatever I did, I could be successful. A few years later, it was clear it was not going to be that simple. Being honest with myself, I felt like I had failed at my goal of playing basketball on a professional level and providing a quality life for Seretha and our family, but I was not ready to give up, because I had an education and had my best friend and love by my side. Having just gotten married, I needed something more stable, so I didn't have to leave my wife to chase a dream that may or may not come true. It was also God's will and blessings.

Seretha had checked herself into the hospital around this time because she was having some anxiety issues with all that had taken place during the course of 1972. The experience of finding blood family and wanting to spend time with them, getting married, and my wife's feelings about all of that were taking a toll. Despite feeling like I could still play basketball at a high level, I followed my priorities. I had to do the important things for our life together away from the game.

I chose to enter the Jefferson County School System as a teacher and coach at Louisville Male High School Track and Cross Country as an assistant coach, a time of my life that you'll hear more about in later chapters. But 1972 wasn't over yet.

In that first meeting with my father, he expressed interest in us getting back together and exploring the family tree deeper. About a week later, he returned to visit, bringing my older brother, Theodore Penebaker, Jr., and his wife and infant son. My brother Theodore and I shared the same mother and father, and I was very excited to meet him.

In that meeting, I again saw that my father was aggressive without emotional constraints.

Still, we proceeded to put the pieces together. My father had already said he didn't know about me and my brother Theodore had never heard of me, either. For my part, I had known that I had a father and brothers and sisters. Beyond that, there were only questions. *Were my mother and father still together, or had they separated? Who were my siblings? What were their names and ages?* Now, I was starting to get answers, finally meeting the people in real life who had for so long only lived as ideas in my mind. A short while after that visit, my wife and I even went to Cincinnati, Ohio, where my father lived, to meet with his wife (a wonderful person), my brothers and sister, and their families. On this trip to visit everyone, my father asked if I wanted to change my name back to Penebaker, to which I responded very quickly, "No way!" He understood, but at the time I had no idea where the response came from. I had to honor the woman and family who had raised me, who had provided me a home, and allowed me to carry the Tinsley name.

Soon after that meeting with my father, and after speaking with Mary—who finally started to give me a little more information once my father showed up—I was able to get a phone number for my mother.

I called, and one of my brothers answered. I told him who I was. He knew the name, and when he heard who I was, I could hear a lot of screaming and hollering through the house.

"Mama, George Tinsley is on the phone," my brother called out. "He says you're his mama, and he's our brother." She came to the phone and was quite emotional. She did most of the talking while I listened. She said that back when I was a baby, after dropping me off at Mama Tinsley's, she had tried to find me but couldn't. All kinds of emotions ran through me. Growing up, this is what I'd always wanted: to know who my mother was and meet my brothers and sisters.

The story I had heard about my mother going off and leaving me had angered me and therefore I was not ready to be understanding from the beginning. Reconnecting now was draining and exciting all at once. I learned that after I was left with Mama Tinsley as a baby, she had been a babysitter for lots of mothers in the area. I was just one of the children she kept.

My understanding from Mama Tinsley's son Clarence was that he and my mother dated for a short period, and he thought that I was his son due to that fact. I was told by my sister Mary that my mother went to Cincinnati, Ohio, to look for my father. My older brother was there with him. Mama and I were moving around from place to place due to the fact that she could not afford to pay rent consistently. We wound up living for several years just outside of the city in Harrods Creek, staying with her family in the family home. Different family members who were going through tough times would be allowed to stay there until they were able to move out. I was there until school started when I was almost six years old. When she returned, my mother said she looked for me and couldn't find me. At this stage, I don't want to say that she abandoned me, left me, and didn't return. Whatever happened is in the past, and only she and Mama Tinsley knew the facts—everything else was hearsay.

There came a point in time when I met with both my biological parents at my mother-in-law's home. This meeting was to clear up everything that had happened. My father stood strong and clearly stated that he knew nothing about me being born or that he had another son. My mother disputed the claim and indicated that my father was very abusive, and she was not able to communicate things with him.

This denial on both sides escalated to a high emotional level where I had to stop the two of them to proclaim that it really did not matter to me anymore. I had found my father, mother, and siblings. I was satisfied with that, and it really did not matter moving forward because I did not need either of them. I just wanted to get to know my brothers and sister if they wanted to have a relationship. In particular, I wanted to form a relationship with my older brother, because we shared the same mother and father. By this point, I was reasonably successful and knew that I could make it in life.

Having my family in my life suddenly left me feeling a mix of relief and many concerns. I was heartened by finally getting answers to questions that had hung in my mind for many years, but I was not at all ready to believe everything I was being told. As someone who had spent much of his life alone, I was suddenly connected to a lot of family, and that left me with even more questions and emotions. I was anxious about this circle of newly discovered relatives. I wondered how all of this would affect my connections with Mama's family—the family that raised me, the only true family who was always there for me through thick and thin.

As excited as I was to have finally reconnected with my blood family, primarily my brothers and sisters on both sides, the family that had raised me would always be in my heart and soul. Mama had long since left the earth, but Mary was very much a part of my life. She had been somewhat of an anchor for me throughout my growing up, and I was very close with her. There was also Mama's son, Clarence, who had taken me in at thirteen after Mama passed. He and his wife had raised me through high school and into college.

I had nieces and nephews, too—my sister's children—and I had become somewhat of a surrogate father to them. I helped my sister take care of them as much as I could during their youth. They were important people in my life. At one point, I sat down with them to talk about what was happening with me finding my family. My sister was not thrilled, but she was understanding, and she loved and supported me.

Clarence was a totally different story because he felt that he was actually likely to be my father—given that he and my mother dated for a while. It was clear to me that he was not my father, but he had filled that role during my formative years as best he could. Balancing my emotions between the two families became something of a mental challenge and a drain. I had the Tinsleys, who knew me well. And the new family(s) who wanted to get to know me. I did my best to build and maintain close ties with both sides as well as I could.

Decades later the consequences of those moving events in 1972 are still with me. My marriage has been the central force of my life ever since. My career decisions that year have defined much of my life, and I am still in contact with all my remaining brothers and sisters on both sides and have nothing but love for each of them. There was and always will be a lot to unpack for each individual involved. Therefore, I cannot expect everyone to clearly understand and accept what happened. We are not the perfect family, but we are family—three families.

Many of the critical members of my family are now deceased. That includes my mother and father, Mama, my sister Mary, Clarence, and Olivia Tinsley. I have also lost a sister on my mother's side, and a sister and a brother on my father's side. Over time, I think that the survivors of the family that raised me—Mary's children—have come to feel that I stepped away from them. I am hopeful that time fixes those issues that exist.

I have maintained a closeness with one of my nieces on that side of the family, Dr. Rana Johnson, vice president at Kansas State University. She and I probably talk more than anybody else on that side of the family. I am very proud of her accomplishments and how she looks out for her siblings. She gives me an insight into where the other brothers and sisters are and their perspectives on our relationships.

On the other hand, I have a very good relationship with the cousins and other relatives who were Mama's relatives in Harris Creek, where we grew up. They're very proud of my success. And one of my cousins played a big part in my life from the KFC standpoint. I helped him get a franchise. And when the opportunity came, he stepped up and supported me. He was in a financial position to be able to help, and I was very grateful for that.

On a national and international level, 1972 was marked by several high-profile events. It was the year of the Munich massacre, when terrorists killed eleven members of the Israeli Olympic team in the Munich Summer Games. It was also the year that *The Godfather* was a hit on the big screen. And it was also a big election year with Richard Nixon being elected president.

Quite a year to remember!

I will always remember 1972 for the personal experiences it brought me. Although each of these events of my life in 1972 was separate, with time, it struck me that there was a crucial tie between them. The career change, the discovery of my family, and, of course, my marriage were all roads that led me to the same destination: an understanding that family was and always will be the driving force in my life.

TEACHING

After departing the ABA, I started teaching and coaching at Male High School, my alma mater, in Louisville. I joined as a substitute teacher in the middle of the year, teaching anatomy and physiology. I became an assistant coach, too, with the cross-country team, track and field, and the following year with the basketball team.

In some ways, that was an easy transition. As an alumnus, I was familiar with the school and knew some administrators. I particularly liked engaging with the kids as a teacher and coach. But some aspects of Male had significantly changed in the seven or eight years since I graduated. The relationship between teachers and students was dramatically different. In my day, students showed respect and deference to their teachers and coaches. Usually, the word of the adults in the room was the final word. Once teachers announced a decision or asked a question, the student refrain was "Yes, sir, yes, ma'am; no, sir, no, ma'am."

When it came to sports, little had changed from my day. On the playing field, there was still respect between athletes and coaches, and going from playing professional ball to coaching turned out to be an excellent experience. Working with other coaches, I was able to motivate youngsters in sports. Because I had a reputation, kids would listen to someone who had been there and had the experience. It helped that I was still young enough to quickly jump onto the court, the cross-country trail, or on the track and demonstrate how to do things. And we had winning teams! In the basketball program, we were runners-up in the state championship our very first year together. We won State the very next year. A good friend, Wade Houston, was the head coach, and I functioned as an assistant cohead coach. Wade allowed me to be an integral part of the coaching decisions.

My experience in the classroom was more problematic. The classroom environment was not as respectful because students were more casual. They were playful and talked back. Kids called teachers by their first names—something that would have never happened in my student days. The dress code had all but deteriorated. These changes called for me to make significant adjustments in my approach.

In my student days, teachers used tools to discipline those who acted up. They could send kids to the principal's office, use a paddle, or take other measures. But when I became a teacher, there was no paddling or real way to push back against kids who talked back to you. The only option was to send the kids to the office. And the office would send them right back to the classroom. No parental engagement, parent-teacher conferences, or any of those things were going on. The student discipline system went from bad to worse during my three years of classroom teaching.

I had one particularly bad experience during my third year as a teacher. I had a student-athlete taking a gym class, fulfilling a school requirement. After gym, students had to shower to prepare for the next class. But this young man decided that he was not going to take a shower. "Hey," I told him, "you're gonna shower or have to take a lick with the paddle." While paddling wasn't allowed in the classroom, we could do it in the gym, and particularly with our players.

"I'm not going to take a shower," he responded. "And you're not going to give me a lick with the paddle or anything else.

"I got something for you," he added.

Standing there, facing off against an agitated student, I realized this was a potentially volatile situation. I had to call on my best mediator instincts to get past this. The only way I knew to defuse the situation was to kick him out of class. Then I called the office.

He stood across the hall and repeated his threat. "I got something for you," he said again.

The next day, I came to school prepared for a confrontation. Fortunately, the school administration intervened and headed off a standoff. But then, not too long after, the school district began to initiate a forced busing regime.

The white and Black kids were required to take buses to different parts of the city to help bring about integration. I was moved to another school for my teaching job but could remain at Male High School for my coaching responsibilities. My commute to school required me to drive through a neighborhood where antibusing protests occurred. I witnessed the picketing and chanting and, above all, the anger. As a coach, I was required to get to school early to help guard the students as they were entering the building.

A NEW LIFE

The standoff with the student and the tensions over busing led me to understand that teaching was not the best career path for me. We were also graduating our very best players and losing others to busing. However, I could always find ways to engage in mentoring a younger generation of athletes. Looking back, another significant factor that played a role in my decision to leave education was the call of my personal and family life.

During my years of teaching, Seretha and I had gotten married. She became pregnant and transitioned jobs to work with her father in the radio business. This was a business that she had grown up in, and she loved the business. Then, my daughter, Penni, came along in 1976, my final year of teaching and coaching. That helped me make my decision from a salary standpoint that I had to start thinking about not so much enjoying what I was doing but understanding that I had to improve my financial situation.

I had to consider a new set of obligations and responsibilities. The sacrifices I had made as a single man—accepting a lower salary, living in a rental apartment, and so on—no longer made sense. The questions about my birth family that had plagued me for years also needed answering. Although I did not fully realize it then, my need to focus on these aspects of life undoubtedly influenced my decision to forge a different career.

During that time, many FBI agents were being forced into early retirement. I had been recruited; therefore, I applied, went through the whole process, and got offered the job to go to Quantico, Virginia, where they were based, to train. They offered a salary of $14,500, which was a significant jump for me. While I was mulling over the opportunity, I went to work at the Kentucky State Fairgrounds as an event coordinator.

It was an interim job move, but I made significantly more than teaching. I was in charge of the Freedom Hall exhibit space, where the University of Louisville basketball teams played. Also, I had a leadership role in the Kentucky State Fairgrounds and a big part in contract negotiations. I used to carry a thesaurus and dictionary in my jacket pockets to help me work through these contracts and understand many of the business terms. I was not ashamed to admit it!

A representative from the FBI came to our home and met with my wife, me, and our daughter. He explained the requirements for joining the agency. We could not come back within six hundred miles of our homes, and all our telephone calls would be monitored. While the financial offer was more exciting, I was not too cool with all the risk factors.

As I plotted my next career step, I worried about the requirements imposed by the FBI and about abruptly moving my new family. I realized that I didn't have to start a new career search from scratch. Especially in Kentucky, my earlier successes opened doors. Once those doors were opened, it was game on. Whatever job came my way, I knew I could transfer many of the skills that I learned in playing sports, including all of the trial and error and eventual triumph I had experienced.

At the time, a friend named Walt Simon who I'd played professional basketball with was working with KFC. I had told him one day while we were playing ball what I was doing and the options I was looking at. He suggested I come out and interview for a job at KFC and possibly work for him. During that interview process with many departments, including human resources, a training position emerged. I eventually took that offer as a trainer, and it would morph into a career.

I would pursue this Kentucky Fried Chicken Corporate (KFCC) and franchising career for the following five decades with great success. Little did I know that I would be working with Colonel Harland Sanders for the next three years.

CHAPTER SIX

BURNING AMBITION

After my second year with KFCC, I'd earned a reputation as a corporate team player who got things done. I became a problem solver for many franchisees who had clout with leadership within the franchise department. They would ask KFC whether I could come into their market to help them resolve some issues.

Although I had never run a restaurant or been in operations, I'd had enough KFC management training to articulate the basics of running a restaurant in classroom-style settings. When owners requested me to help resolve issues, the doors would open in other areas of the corporate and franchise side of the business due to the results that I produced.

When I was up for a promotion, I received many offers for management-level jobs in different cities. These offers would be big moves with the family outside of the city and state. My daughter Penni was born, and my wife was pregnant with our son, George, coming soon. I had to consider these opportunities financially, along with location and career development. In the corporate structure, it was unwise to turn down offers too many times lest you risk getting labeled as someone who was not willing to grow.

But by that time, we had two kids—Penni and George II—and Seretha and I were managing our new family. I was also nervous about leaving Louisville, giving up my comfort zone, and uprooting my family. After talking it through with Seretha, I opted to go to Atlanta and become an area supervisor. That meant stepping into operations and becoming a supervisor for seven restaurants. It also called for resettling my family in a new city.

For two years I was an area supervisor. Although I was new to this kind of role, I stepped lively into it. Among other things, it got me involved with the sales profits and evaluations of the businesses. I also started developing training programs for people who were moving out of the restaurants into area supervisor positions.

Soon came another promotion, this time to district training manager. I continued operations and managed a KFC training store based in Atlanta. Fortunately, Seretha had landed a great job as general manager of an Atlanta radio station. As I racked up successes, the work I was doing started to get attention in the company. The KFCC office began highlighting the training programs I put together and other things we did in Atlanta in different parts of the country.

That, in turn, led me to another promotion—director of human resources for two of KFC's regions. The good news was that the job brought me and the family back to Louisville. We had a good family support network there and Seretha's mother could help take care of the kids. But the job also called for me to travel frequently. I was helping oversee markets in Dallas, Houston, Los Angeles, San Francisco, Las Vegas, and different parts of Kansas and Hawaii. I would leave every Monday and return home on Thursday or Friday. Being constantly on the road made for a hectic life.

Along the way, I had a chance to meet and work with Colonel Sanders, the founder of the KFC Cooking Process and original owner of KFC. Since joining KFCC, the company, from a distance, I had admired this iconic figure and man. Although his picture, with that signature white hair and whiskers, made him an international celebrity, he was still an enigma in the company. From the first day of work at KFCC, I was like a sponge for anything and everything to do with the company and its products. I sought to absorb and learn all the techniques I could about cooking chickens KFC style. I would take pots and things home and try to recreate the brand products on my home stove. I tried to get the shortening to 375 and 400 degrees to go through this process. For a while, I felt like I was eating and sleeping KFC. I justified it as a preparation for being the very best instructor.

"STILL MAKING BUCKETS"

When the Colonel and I finally met at the new KFC Training Center at Sullivan College, I was awestruck. I had been working for KFC for about three months, and the construction of the KFC training facility at Sullivan Business College had been recently completed. Standing before me was the real person who started the KFC business, developed the recipe, and helped a corporate empire.

In that first meeting, which was arranged by the public relations and marketing department, we took pictures together and engaged in casual conversation. We spent most of the time doing a public relations promo. The company capitalized on my status as a former Kentucky Colonel professional athlete and Louisville Male High School teacher in the Louisville area. They photographed me with a Kentucky Fried Chicken bucket and the Colonel. "Tinsley still making buckets" was the title.

It was a relaxed meeting. The first thing he said to me was, "Boy, you are a fine specimen." I found the comment amusing. The racial climate in the area in the mid-1970s was not as bad as it had been in the 1960s. *Roots*, the popular TV series about Black history based on the novel by the writer Alex Haley, was getting a lot of widespread attention at the time and raising awareness of African American culture, so I took Colonel Sanders's comments positively. But at the same time, they logged a message in my mind about the manner of the man that I was dealing with and where his mindset might be. I just considered where he grew up and came from and played it by ear moving forward. There was a lot of racial history surrounding Corbin, Kentucky, where the Colonel got started. As high school basketball players, we had played the local Corbin high school and were not allowed to get off the bus to eat due to the racial climate.

As we were meeting in a very public setting, in front of many people, I figured out quickly how to keep the flow of conversation in a neutral space, avoiding any sensitive topics. Although I was not easily starstruck after meeting with the Colonel, I felt I had to respect the man and the myth per my position of just starting a new job.

While my growth in the company had been moving along smoothly and I had been promoted several times in operations and training, there were some wrinkles to come. One big one came after I had been promoted to the regional director of human resources for two regions. One of the regional vice presidents decided to bring on a new regional human resource person for his region alone. She was a beautiful, tall, blonde, white woman based in Los Angeles. I actually helped hire her, and we would essentially be doing the same job.

At that time, my salary was about $45,000 a year, with a bonus. But then I found out that her starting salary was $85,000. That dramatic salary difference upset me, given that I had been running two regions and she would only be running one. Keeping in mind that she lived and worked solely on the West Coast, where the cost of living was much higher, I was still very upset.

After careful consideration, I decided to explore franchise ownership options. My wife had recently received an offer to become the vice president of radio station WPDQ in Jacksonville, Florida, and so it was an introspective time for me and our family, deciding what we would do next. With increasing corporate opportunities for minorities in operations and franchising, ownership seemed like the next logical step in my career, and something I could do anywhere Seretha followed her own dreams. So, I decided to take a vacation and enrolled in the Burger King Franchise Lease program and qualified to become a franchisee in their leasing program.

After my vacation, I returned to KFCC and informed my boss that I was leaving to become a Burger King Franchisee. The president of KFCC asked to meet with me and proposed an offer to become a franchise manager with eventual opportunities to become a KFC Franchisee. He sent me to meet with the head of the franchising department, Bill Evans.

Bill Evans, one of the corporate senior vice presidents, asked me to hang in there. "Some opportunities are coming up, and we want to position you to take advantage of them," he said. There was talk of some possible franchisee opportunities. Evans was someone I had come to know and trust as a straight shooter. He was also a former basketball player whom everyone spoke highly of.

Not long after that, corporate offered me the opportunity to become the franchise manager in southern Georgia and northern Florida. Evans was the one who proposed the job. He was the senior VP of franchising and a former professional basketball player who had played for the University of Kentucky.

He and I had developed a relationship because of our sports backgrounds. We knew one another personally and had bonded. He believed in me. His regional vice president, Chuck Reynolds, was also an athlete—a big, muscular guy, a former wrestler who was no nonsense and straightforward. He also expressed faith in my abilities and what I could bring to their department, especially in taking on this new territory. Given the offer and the territory proposed in Jacksonville, my wife and I both accepted our new positions, and once again, we pulled up stakes and moved to Florida.

A PISTOL ON THE TABLE

Early in that position, we convened a lunch meeting of the franchisees I would be supervising. They did not hide their displeasure at having me in charge. One of the franchise owners came with his gun. I am not sure if this was meant as a means of intimidation or something else. In any case, he set it on the table for me, my supervisor, and the other franchise attendees to see.

He was visibly uncomfortable, pushed his food away, turned red in the face, and declined to make eye contact with me. I had been informed that there were members of the Ku Klux Klan or other white supremacists possibly in the group and a mood of anxiety hung heavy in the air. All except for one of the ten owners of franchises under my jurisdiction were white men. There was also one white female who attended the lunch.

My supervisors called the meeting to update the franchises on significant corporate rule changes and introduce me as their new supervisor. Other contractual topics were to be discussed and agreed upon as KFCC Franchise Contractual agreements. As I surveyed the room, my mind fixated on the racial dynamic and what I had learned earlier about the mood of me coming into the area. It struck me that this was likely the first time any of the owners had had a corporate representative who was Black. The nondescript setting—a conference room in a Jacksonville, Florida, hotel—belied the owners' hostile attitude.

I knew in the run-up to the meeting that there would be issues. Through the corporate grapevine, I learned that several franchisees had some serious racial issues. Some had called the corporate offices to say they did not want to work with me. They proposed that the KFC management bring a white franchise manager who lived and worked in the South Carolina area to come in and help. Another option they had suggested was hiring a white supervisor from South Florida, a different territory. The KFC home office had rejected the alternative suggestions and stayed behind the decision to make me district manager.

Such was the mood in the southern United States in the 1970s. The Civil Rights Movement, which had forced changes in education, housing, and other areas, now required companies to further integrate and promote Black employees into their corporate ranks who were performing well. KFC's corporate and its parent company, R. J. Reynolds, had begun to heed the call to increase and promote Black representation in the company.

One of the people who was exhorting the company and others to lift up the profile of Blacks was Reverend Jesse Jackson. He and Operation Push, his organization, had begun to push corporate America to open up opportunities for ownership of certain franchises, along with promotion opportunities for Black executives in senior corporate positions. Since KFCC was a company with a large Black clientele, these steps were essential for them to keep good relations with their customers. KFC at the time was owned by the R. J. Reynolds Company, which was very sensitive about different issues that were within and impacted the organization. KFC at the time only had two Black franchisees in the system.

As a new district franchise manager, I was still learning the franchising part of the business. That first meeting was, in a sense, a challenge of my mettle. Could I defuse the tensions, work through the franchise issues, and help their franchises thrive? As we entered the meeting, these were among the questions in the air.

MORE CHALLENGES

Fortunately, I had a solid record in all my other positions with KFC and being a former professional athlete did not hurt from opening the door for conversation. The home office, keenly aware of the issues the franchises had, was working on solutions. I later discovered that they had been trying to find and carve out an area where I would be comfortable in South Georgia and North Florida. And for good reason. There were only a few Black franchisees in the nation and none in that area, but the customer base was heavily Black. This was an opportunity for the beginning of a movement for KFCC operations, franchising development, and franchise ownership.

Upon assuming my role as the district franchise manager, I embarked on a tour to engage with various franchise owners one-on-one. It soon became evident that I was facing a host of complex situations, particularly in the northern Florida region. Here, not only did I encounter racial tensions, but I also noticed that the franchisees, having operated under the earlier contractual policies set by Colonel Sanders's family, had developed a tendency to deviate from stringent operational protocols.

At that stage, I had worked in KFC's corporate office for five years, inching my way up the company ladder. The path I took, moving from one position to the next, always further up the management tree, helped me build strong relations among senior KFC staff. It didn't hurt that I spent time with KFC founder Colonel Sanders either, something I'll talk about more in a minute. There were not many KFC team members at any level who had had direct time with Colonel Sanders as I had. It gave me a certain cachet, storylines, and bragging rights.

As a newcomer to the corporate world, I had to make some adjustments from my earlier careers in sports and teaching. The basics of my new job—getting up in front of a group and making presentations—came easily enough. By then, I was steady on my feet appearing before audiences. But I did not know the KFC business, its mission, and its inner workings. As I had become accustomed to doing in new situations, I dove into the company and the job, dedicating myself to learning more about how KFCC worked politically, what my job entailed, and what the superiors expected of me. As with any new workplace situation, it took me a while to adjust along with finding several mentors. Naturally, the more awareness I had about the company's inner workings and the KFCC culture, the more confident I became.

By then, it was transparent to me about how the jobs worked: if I didn't deliver what was expected, they could always get rid of me. From the start, I liked the job and the prospects and was determined to do all I could to succeed and grow in the company. During this learning phase, the discipline I had learned in my career as an athlete and teacher/coach kicked in. Just as I had learned how to improve my offensive skills on the basketball court or to muster my techniques in track and field, I had to dig into whatever it took to be the best possible KFCC trainer with the brands of H Salt Sea Food and Zantigo, a Mexican American concept.

And just as there had been on the basketball court or other sports playing fields, there was a sense of competition between me and my KFC training instructor colleagues. The company had hired six trainers, and we were all eager to meet the job's demands and succeed. The competition was high, primarily because our training department was new to the organization, and the overall business of KFC had begun a slide in revenues system-wide. As a new, non-revenue-producing department, as I mentioned earlier, we had to produce to justify our existence.

The first crunch came about two months into the job when corporate decided to make some cuts in the training program. Everybody was nervous about their job security, and it was nerve-wracking not knowing what was going to happen. In the end, there were layoffs, but I survived them. I was one of the true trainers who had a teaching background and who did not have to relocate to the home office. I also was the only trainer who could teach the train-the-trainer classes.

BUILDING TRUST

Leaving the meeting, I knew that this peace between me and the franchisees was temporary. A couple of them still didn't want to shake hands or deal with me at all. If I was going to succeed in my role as their liaison between KFCC and franchising their business while helping them succeed and grow, I had my work cut out for me.

My modus operandi in almost all such challenging missions is to first go through a discovery process to find out who and what personalities and issues I was dealing with. It was no different in this case. I had to scope out who the franchisees were, how their businesses were doing, and develop a strategy. I did a lot of visiting of the different franchise restaurants, particularly in northern Florida. I went on my own, as a customer, incognito.

I focused on one franchisee in particular. I chose him because he was a leader, and the largest owner in the group. I tried to understand how his operation worked and what I could do to make him more successful. I talked to some of the employees during my visits as if I were a true customer and potential employee. To them, I was another customer. I popped in, bought lunch, and asked a few questions, always with the purpose of understanding where I could be the most effective. He had two supervisors, and they were easier to work with and took suggestions. These suggestions helped them make bonus for themselves and their managers.

From there, I pulled all the information together that I had gathered. I could, by this point in my career, analyze the business from the time I pulled into the parking lot, walked in the front door, and typically headed straight to the restrooms, lastly moving to the front counter and observing the mood of employees, their overall approach to customer service, and the product being sold.

At that stage, I was ready to meet with the franchisees. I set up one-on-one meetings with them. I chose the first franchise visit with the franchise mentioned earlier as the most influential in the group. My objective was to share some suggestions that would help him increase revenues and grow his business. One point that helped me in those meetings was, again, that I had worked with the Colonel and learned his success secrets, "the golden rule of customer service." That gave me high credentials.

Secondly, being a former professional athlete became a talking point to break the ice in most conversations as a lead-in. My stature, at six-five and 225 pounds, helped, and I was able to articulate and offer frank business acumen while truly listening to their concerns.

Drawing from my earlier background in training also enabled me to assist them in working through some of the business challenges they were facing.

Above all, I was telling them that I wanted to show them ways they could drive sales higher and increase revenues. I explained how to increase their bottom line through improved operations, pricing, product marketing, and product controls in place. I offered some tips on how to run a better operation in the kitchen and elsewhere in the restaurant. As I spoke, I was careful to ensure they were not intimidated or turned off as a Mr. Know-it-all. I assured them I was not there as a corporate representative looking to begin the process of pulling their franchise agreements or infringing on their operations in any way.

In these conversations, it helped me to imagine myself in their position. The fact that I was a Black man added another factor of concern to some of these franchisees. One franchise felt very clearly that I was going to give him a very tough time due to his feelings about race.

So, it was up to me to demonstrate that I was not a corporate person coming to beat people up. I was not going to report back to senior leadership about the improper things that might have been done, like keeping chickens out longer than they were supposed to or violating other rules. We were going to fix these things together and, by doing so, show them how to improve guest satisfaction and improve customer traffic, which was going to increase revenues with repeat business.

I just showed them how to do things better and how to employ tactics to increase their customer bases. My goal was to demonstrate how they could make more money. That was the bottom line. My message and the way I delivered it seemed to resonate.

In most cases, I could see that the owners began to see me differently and invited me back to their restaurants more frequently for unofficial visits. They looked beyond my skin color and judged me by my character, overcoming their earlier fears that a person from corporate was coming into their restaurant. They would then go back and tell all the negative things that were going on.

That's something that people look for in developing relationships: a person who maintains their calm and practices what they preach in stressful situations. I think what came through was my KFC knowledge and character. I believed in what I was doing, so I convinced them that this was the right way to do things. There wasn't any talking from both sides of my mouth as some other franchise managers had done in the past. I also didn't mind getting in the trenches with them and helping out during busy times.

That approach opened the doors of communication between us. What would happen is that I was able to help one franchisee start to turn around their sales, get increased customer engagement, and so on. Then they would share with another franchisee, "Hey, this guy knows what he's doing, and he's bringing people in from the corporate office in Louisville to the market to help with training sessions. He associates with us, and he's not a negative person. He's not coming in with the Black power attitude or any of that kind of stuff." I think those kinds of conversations among franchisees continued to open doors. Over time, they all got on board with my KFC program of doing things the Colonel's way.

One franchisee took about nine months to become comfortable with me. He had eight restaurants and continually came up with all kinds of excuses not to meet with me, sending some of his subordinates to meetings instead of attending himself. Franchise managers should usually meet with franchisees once every three months. If there was a significant problem, the meeting would occur sooner. With the other franchisees, I made it a point to meet with them at least once a quarter.

Twice a year, in the summer and fall, we called a Southeastern KFC Association franchise meeting in Atlanta, where all the franchisees in the southeast would come together for a three-day meeting with each other and potential distributors sponsoring the event. KFCC executives of franchising were a part of these meetings, and we were encouraged to invite our franchisees and representatives to the meeting. The Florida franchisees rarely attended these meetings prior to my coming into the area.

To my credit, several of my franchisees attended initially, and within time, 90 percent attended. They all came except the two who had significant issues. But the rest came, and I got to meet and get to know them in a more relaxed setting. These guys were competitive with each other and didn't want one to get ahead of the other.

I would also have meetings in Jacksonville or South Georgia and invite the franchisees to cover different topics. Eventually, the franchisees saw the positive actions I was taking, bringing people in from corporate and exposing them to other areas and opportunities. They saw I was focused on showing them ways of growing their business and making more money. It all became a hit with the franchisees. Even the franchisees who had real issues started coming to meetings. Many of these guys were relatives and knew one another, and they started talking about how much they enjoyed working with me.

A TURN FOR THE BETTER

At the end of the first year after that initial, tense meeting, we held our own regional gathering. This time, all the franchisees came, including the two who were holdouts and initially declined to work with me. They pulled themselves in, and we took a picture together, arms around one another. While we were never buddy-buddy and going to each other's homes to hang out for dinner, we did grow closer and it became a lot easier to work with the entire group. I stayed in this role for three years and developed great relationships with the franchisees.

During this time frame, I was also instrumental in helping several Black franchisees in South Georgia with their business. Milton Sanders in Tifton, Georgia and Brady Keys located in Albany, Georgia. Brady was a very strong franchisee, and he and Donald Lopes of Rhode Island were two of the very first Black franchisees in the KFC system. Brady relocated his business to South Georgia with a swap of his Detroit holdings there with KFCC. He did not need as much support from me. I actually learned from him as he made his business a big part of the community.

Along with Brady, Milton, Martin Dunbar in Kentucky, Ronald Johnson in New York, Lois Foust in Los Angeles, Peter Ebbs in Cincinnati, Ohio, and several other franchisees in the northeast, I helped them start the Minority Franchisee Association. I later became a part of the leadership group when I became a franchisee in Florida.

Aside from the assistance I was able to give to the franchisees, my three years as a district manager were a crash course for me in franchise management. I had encountered every possible dilemma a franchisee could face in their business. These three years as a district manager in the franchising department positioned me perfectly for the next chapter of my KFC life as a franchisee. I truly felt that since I had assisted these franchisees in building their businesses and I'd seen them become multimillionaires, I could do it myself if I ever had the opportunity to do so. My goal since joining KFC Corporation in the training department was to one day own my own franchise and provide a better life for my family. I always felt that working with a franchisor like KFC YUM and using their resources combined with my dedication, leadership skills, community involvement, and family values would lead to tremendous success. I could also help others make a comfortable living. And it would be more profitable personally owning my own franchise business than working for the corporation. I enjoyed my work as a corporate employee, but I had an opportunity to make millions while taking on the American Dream. I had to work through any obstacles so I could seize it. Once I left, I would no longer work for KFC Corporation. That opportunity was just around the door, as you'll hear more about in the next chapter.

During one southeastern meeting, I sat at a table with all the regional vice presidents. We were all eating and drinking adult beverages. Some had more than they could handle and started talking about confidential information not yet to be discussed with all employees. KFCC was starting a minority guaranteed financing program due to the pressure that was being put on KFCC and the R. J. Reynolds Corporation who owned KFCC at the time. One of the VPs leaned over to me and suggested that I might apply for one of these franchise opportunities, given my track record and success within the business.

Upon leaving the meeting, I went back to my room and drafted a letter to the VP of franchising and to Bill Evans about the opportunity to become a minority franchisee in the South. Bill Evans was not too happy that I had found out and that I had written a letter response to that VP and copied him. We had a long discussion, which ended in the fact that if anything ever came up in Florida, I would be the first to know and be considered. As I mentioned earlier, Bill was a man of his word. While taking a year or so, that opportunity did open up for three possible territories of the Disney area, South

Miami, and Auburndale, Florida, which was the most cost-effective area of the three.

My wife resigned from her job in the radio business, which she absolutely loved, and we packed up the two children and moved to Winter Haven, Florida. I had done extensive research on all three offers, and the Auburndale offer made the most sense financially. We borrowed money from my cousin and my father-in-law, and put our own savings, which all combined came up to a 20 percent down payment on the KFCC-backed guaranteed loan for development of the very first restaurant. We stayed in the Holiday Inn until we found and purchased a home in Winter Haven, while developing our first KFC in Auburndale. This was a six-month period of development with very few problems.

CHAPTER SEVEN

AN ENTREPRENEURIAL EMPIRE

My family and I had built a solid restaurant empire from scratch by the time I reached my sixth decade. It's an achievement that, as a kid growing up in hardscrabble Smoketown, Louisville, I could have never imagined. Our first company was named PenGeo Inc. doing business as KFC. The name came from Penni and George, the first three letters in each of their names. Our second company, representing the four KFC restaurants in the Tampa Bay area (which began in the bottom one hundred of KFC restaurants targeted for sale via the Minority Franchising Program was SerGeo Inc. for Seretha and George, after which Seretha made me promise to never name another company after her!

So our first business in the Tampa airport, TGI Fridays, was under the name Tinsley Group, and comprised Clarence Daniels, PenGeo Inc., DBA/KFC, and myself. We also had a TGI Fridays in Lakeland, Florida, under the Tinsley Family business. Our future businesses in airports and other opportunities were all under the later Tinsley Family Concessions business umbrella.

Tinsley Family Concessions, Inc., the family's flagship company, operated sixty franchise and licensed restaurants at our height. The company now controls forty-five licensed concession restaurants, subleases, and joint ventures combined. Our operations center on food and beverage businesses. In addition, we have retail establishments in the Miami International Airport. They include full-service restaurants like PF Chang's, Chili's, KFC, Starbucks, Shula's Bar & Grill, Burger King, Pei Wei, the Bourbon Academy & Tasting Room, Cigar City Bar & Restaurant, and other branded and nonbranded concepts in various airports. The businesses' total revenues have been successful and solidly above the norm.

In early 2023, we made vital changes in the leadership of Tinsley Family Concessions. My son, George Tinsley II, took on the role of the company's president by purchasing the majority of controlling shares. I became cofounder and vice president, and my wife, Seretha, has remained a cofounder, secretary, and treasurer. It's a great moment of transition in the legacy of the business that the Tinsley family has built together. Now I can turn things over to my son's control.

After devoting decades to taking advantage of opportunities to create and broaden the business, it's been refreshing to step back from the daily hands-on operations and watch my son apply his management and leadership style. I engage whenever necessary while giving George II room to grow the company as he develops his legacy.

My newfound role has also given me time to make a comprehensive account of the business. It has allowed me to take stock of the lives that we have touched, developed, and motivated to be the best they can be in life, no matter their choices moving forward. We have employed a third generation of employees and, in one case, a fourth-generation employee. Among the alumni of our businesses, there are medical doctors, doctors in education, lawyers, judges, ministers, elected officials, professional athletes, NBA executives, and college coaches. They all started their careers in one of our businesses and bounded forward. This group of "Tinsley business graduates," coupled with giving back to the community, has been a tremendous reward for our hard work over the last nearly forty years.

The year 2024 finds the company in solid shape. We're almost debt-free, and we don't have to worry about paying one loan as we advance. We've also been able to make investments, including in property, from several homes and buildings throughout the city to our office complex and community development projects that are still moving forward.

As the business grew and I assumed a higher profile as an African American business leader, I took on various corporate and civic positions. My roles ranged from different board member positions to eventually being highlighted as board chairman of the National Basketball Retired Players Association (NBRPA) and then to a post on the board of directors of Winter Haven Hospital.

Seretha has been equally active in civic organizations. She has joined local and national organizations, including becoming the first Black female president of the Winter Haven Chambers of Commerce and assuming a critical position as a board member in our church home, Winter Haven's First Missionary Baptist Church. She's been an active member of the National Coalition of Black Women (NCBW) and in local leadership positions of the NCBW for over twenty-five years.

It's my hope that our journey to arrive at this place of community, stability, and fulfillment will help other business leaders or aspiring entrepreneurs on their own journeys. No matter the path you choose, obstacles will keep coming, and no matter how difficult the way forward is, you must make every effort to transform these challenges into opportunities.

In this chapter, starting with opening our first Kentucky Fried Chicken outlet in Auburndale, Florida, I'll walk you through how we constructed a successful midsized multimillion-dollar restaurant business. I also assess my role in leading and helping rebuild the NBRPA to become what it is today, representing all the NBA, ABA, WNBA, and Globetrotters in the professional basketball world. Throughout my career, I have used my business and basketball experiences to help solve problems and create a positive pathway for others, as you'll see more of in this chapter.

CONTINUING TO GROW

Even before starting the first KFC franchise in Auburndale, Florida, I knew we would not stop with just one restaurant. We were destined to grow and expand. Yet, Seretha and I did not have a master plan for how that expansion would take place. Once we established an early record of success with our first two restaurants, doors for other opportunities started opening. Businesses or business groups offered us the chance to engage with them in new ventures. More offers came forward than we could handle. We had infrastructure constraints and did not want to move too fast. We were in the excellent position of picking and choosing what business investments made sense.

So, Seretha and I took advantage of the business opportunities that we considered most promising. Like all investors, we learned to evaluate the growth potential of any proposed new restaurant investment. It was organic. We used the skill sets I learned during my eight years working with KFC Corporation and the entrepreneurial tools I amassed while working with the KFC franchise community as a business development director.

Even with all that experience, we made mistakes—some minor, others more significant. Fortunately, we learned the importance of acknowledging our errors and owning them. One example is the third KFC we developed in Davenport, Florida. At the time, the area was known as Baseball City, and it was planned to grow by leaps and bounds. After carefully considering the location and potential, we expected it to boom. But instead, we amassed losses in that business. We decided to close, sell that property, and move forward. The obstacles we encountered while starting and operating businesses and how we dealt with them were just as significant. Still, we learned how to bounce back.

The initial obstacle was when our first restaurant—the KFC in Auburndale, Florida—burned to the ground. This occurred when we had two one-million-dollar KFC restaurants with the poorly operating Baseball City/Davenport KFC struggling. The dramatic setback came ten years after we had opened. In that case, we pivoted quickly to make and execute plans to rebuild and reopen the restaurant. We also used our creative resources to provide products to customers in a temporary setting. I developed a KFC delivery truck so I could take the food to the customer while we were rebuilding. I followed the other food trucks in the area to map out their routine and made sure that I beat them to their spots with my KFC on Wheels. I would come back to that burned-down restaurant early evening selling product out of the KFC on Wheels and let the customers know that we were going to reopen shortly. The end of the story was a happy one. We were able to reopen within months. Thanks in part to our improvements, we doubled the revenues in short order. This was a significant obstacle that turned into a tremendous opportunity.

That experience set a tone and example for me and our company in dealing with such hurdles in the future. We tackled the setback in the most positive can-do way. While dealing with it, we dug deep into the life and business lessons I had learned. Despite the trauma caused by seeing our building reduced to ashes, we moved beyond the emotional reaction. We realized that we had to keep going forward quickly to limit our losses. We also reached out for help—to patrons, community institutions, the flagship KFC Corporation offices, and others. Each of these parties played a vital role in our recovery. Together, we were able to turn a dark event into a grand opportunity.

In my initial attempt to enter the airport restaurant field, we encountered another significant roadblock. I was interested in opening a KFC at the airport in Tampa, Florida. KFC Corporation called me about the opportunity to develop a nontraditional KFC there, and a friend connected me with Clarence Daniels, who worked for HMSHost, the master concessionaire at the Tampa airport. Daniels had worked for HMSHost in development and had become an airport concessions operator in Los Angeles himself.

HMSHost is a leading food service company that develops multiple concession restaurants in airports worldwide. Daniels was head of HMSHost's minority development program at one point in his career, and he understood the airport's Concessions Disadvantaged Business program. He flew in, and in two weeks we put together a proposal that typically takes two years to formulate for this type of deal. The KFC we proposed would have been one of several multi-restaurant spaces in the airport. We submitted the bid to the airport, but we lost the bid to another group.

But then, on the way out, Daniels and I stopped at a tiny bar in the airport's main terminal to drink our sorrows and on the bar television was the now infamous O. J. Simpson freeway chase in the white Bronco on a Southern California freeway. "Well," I said, "He's got a lot of worse problems than we have." We laughed.

As we were leaving, we noticed an empty white tablecloth restaurant space right next to the pub where we had stopped. Our faces lit up. This was a space that Maynard Jackson, the former mayor of Atlanta, had bid on but dropped at the last minute. The next day, we called HMSHost, the airport concessionaire, with a question: If we could get a brand like TGI Fridays to open a casual dining concept in the space, would they consider partnering with us?

They said, "Well, let's see what you have."

I contacted TGI Fridays' executives, who showed great interest in also including the neighboring bar in the deal, which would give us an "A" location rather than a "C" location. We kicked it around and finally decided to propose a joint venture with HMSHost, who owned the bar on the corner of the terminal where we drank and cried in our beers. We had 60 percent of the concept. HMSHost would be the minority partner with 40 percent.

I was the operator, given my street-side experience and being a local living in the area. I also understood the business operations side of the plan. Daniels had more knowledge of how the partnerships with HMSHost in airports worked. We collaborated with Jeff Yablun, the local vice president for HMSHost in the area, in developing the concept to present to the Airport Aviation Authority for them to approve. We introduced the TGI Fridays plan in 1995.

The airport approved and we opened TGI Fridays at the Tampa airport later that same year. We conservatively estimated the projected sales to be $3.2 million in annual revenue. The business model was launched to be profitable for all parties and it boomed. First came daily awards for achieving $28,000. Then, we received weekly awards for serving in the $125,000 range. Finally, by year four, we started receiving sales awards for $5 million in annual revenues. We became one of the top TGI Fridays in the nation and remained so from around 2000 through 2016.

Our success at TGI Fridays and our relationships with HMSHost and the Airport Authority opened a new world of opportunities for us. The first big project it led to was a joint venture partnership, an agreement between the Tinsley Family and HMSHost for several more airport locations in Miami and Louisville.

In 2016, every concept in the Tampa airport had to rebid on new ideas and locations with the significant rebuilding of the airport concessions program. We had to pull together all the resources we could. Formulating the deal and making the presentation to the airport authorities was intensive. Part of what added to the complexity was the different restaurant concepts in the package, including PF Chang's, Pei Wei, Wendy's, Starbucks, and many others. Fortunately, the various brands that were approached wanted to be in the airports because it gave them automatic billboard advertising.

In the end, we won the bid. We occupied a bigger footprint in the Tampa airport with our fifteen joint ventures and the sublease of a Wendy's agreement and our empire-building took a significant leap forward. Soon after we entered the Miami airport scene, we acquired twenty-two restaurants as part of a joint venture partnered with HMSHost. Then came an opportunity in Louisville, Kentucky, where we picked up another six restaurants in the airport. From there, we have slowed our development.

We learned several critical lessons during those expansions. One was to not look over our shoulders at setbacks. After losing our initial bid for the KFC in the Tampa airport, we pivoted quickly and developed a winning concept. Second, we appreciated the importance of partnerships. Our work with Clarence Daniels, who brought knowledge of airport restaurant deals we needed, was crucial. We developed the Tinsley Group as a partnership. Perhaps more importantly, with the success of the first TGI Fridays, we forged a strong working arrangement with HMSHost. That, in turn, led us to the gigantic deals in the Tampa, Miami, and Louisville airports. At one stage, our empire included sixty different restaurant units.

From our initial three KFC franchises, within a few years, we were operating more than forty restaurants. With the surge in the size and scope of our business, a new challenge emerged: *How could we maintain our top-ranked record of service and management?* We had achieved much of that high-level record of detailed personal service because of my initial close involvement in the businesses. But with our dramatic scaling up, it was clear that I could no longer be closely involved in day-to-day operations, behind the register one day, cooking the next. At that point, I started playing the role of managing managers. My modus operandi was to visit the restaurants, checking in on the managers regularly. I was in and out.

But, then, during our first five years at the TGI Fridays in the Tampa airport, I spent a lot of time on location, developing the philosophy and ensuring it was pretty large and high volume. I confirmed we were doing things the way I wanted to see them done, along with the brand requirements. I didn't visit the KFC units much and relied on the management teams, the point-of-sale equipment, and camera systems. With those tools, I could closely monitor the ability to be on top of things if something did come up.

We developed strict training programs to ensure competence among managers and all employees. Every new person coming in, hourly or management, had to undergo a training program of at least six weeks. We also introduced and implemented the corporate philosophy through our different human resource activities, such as preopening and end-of-shift meetings. And we had monthly meetings for the management team and quarterly meetings for the staff to discuss how we would approach our guests and other issues.

All the restaurant groups we worked with—from KFC to Starbucks and TGI Fridays—had their well-developed training programs. While many other franchises deviated significantly from the corporate training, we didn't. Sometimes, we added our little touches in cleanliness, quality, and customer satisfaction, but whether it was Chili's or any other brand, we stuck with their program.

Even as our business capacity peaked, I had a rule to appear at all our restaurants at least once a month. Where feasible, I was in at least one of our restaurants daily, including on weekends. I made it happen, even if that involved driving an hour or two or getting on a plane. It didn't make sense for me then to get involved in any business if I could not be there at least once a month.

SIX RULES

During our forty-plus years in business, many other issues came up. One was how to deal with racial biases among customers. Another was the retention of staff and managers. This had never been a problem before but became one during the COVID-19 pandemic. And then our daughter Penni fell ill, requiring me to devote time to her as her primary caregiver. In all these cases, we approached each situation with optimism and the understanding that whatever the obstacle was, there was a way to turn it into an opportunity. Over the years, I have developed a few rules of thumb for this mindset that apply to business operations.

Rule 1: Never buy an existing restaurant. This was a big lesson I learned in purchasing the four restaurants in the Tampa Bay area. Because of historical issues, they were too challenging to make profitable. Building from the ground up versus buying an existing restaurant is always advantageous, because you don't have to turn that business around. I'm not saying to *never* do these deals. But when you buy an existing location with a negative backstory, be aware that it will take a lot to turn it around. That happened with my TGI Fridays in Lakeland, Florida. After two years, we couldn't make it profitable, so we shut it down and sold it back to the corporation. This brings me to Rule 2.

Rule 2: If you can't turn around a business in two years, it's time to get out of it. You must have a system for evaluating the company on a weekly, monthly, and quarterly basis from the standpoint of sales, profits, and opportunities. If you consistently fall short, assess what it will take to turn it around and what it will cost you, whether it's a physical investment or investing in the training, retention, or replacement of people. If that turnaround cannot be achieved in two years, do whatever you must to get out. If you don't, it's going to take you under.

Rule 3: Location is always crucial. I know this has been said before, but I will continue to repeat it. You want to be in a high-traffic area with significant ingress and egress opportunities.

Rule 4: Spend time in the restaurant, talking to customers, listening to their feedback, and driving that personal brand marketing side. I call it Gorilla Focus on community-based marketing. So, as long as you can keep that up, people will return. If you're not there, they return to hope to get a chance to see you and spend some time with you.

Rule 5: Airport restaurant locations require a different marketing approach. With the rush of people coming and going, developing a regular clientele is challenging in airport businesses. You don't get to establish yourself, who you are, or your philosophy. But you can develop good relations with the airport community and the people working there. That's helpful because many people going through airports ask workers for assistance and recommendations. *Where can they eat a good meal in a clean environment? Where do you recommend eating?* Airport employees who know your reputation will refer customers. That helped us with that first TGI Fridays business at the Tampa airport. We got involved in the community at the airport, and this meant the people who worked there were a key part of our word-of-mouth.

Rule 6: Whatever brand you work with, grand openings are crucial. Typically, you open a couple of weeks before, doing test runs, maybe over three days out of the week. Invite all employees and their relatives for a planned meal and let them learn what's happening. Also, invite community leaders, the chamber of commerce, and other groups that are strong in their community, letting them get to know you, see what goes on, and taste some of your products. Then you have a sales and service day where the sales folks meet the employees. And all these are comped meals. Word gets out in the community when you go through this process.

It's essential to have a robust staffing plan in place for your grand opening. Typically, the initial two weeks draw in strong crowds, and you need to ensure that your team is primed to deliver exceptional service to match the high demand and sustain that early surge of interest. Often, businesses reduce their staff numbers after a grand opening, which can lead to a decrease in customer service quality. If customers don't receive the attention they expect, they're likely to take their business elsewhere instead of returning.

There will come a point when you have to evaluate the business weekly to ensure that you keep labor in the right spots. They should be concentrated in the front of the house, primarily supporting the restrooms and parking lot, caring for customers, and getting them in and out. That will continue to keep those people flowing. Then you gradually cut it back, find out where your sweet spot is when some of the newness wears off with the customers, and make that transition inside. That's typically my philosophy on getting through the first six months of the business, which establishes it for moving forward.

When you open, the community will want to try the "new place." Then, they usually leave and tell ten more people. This kind of word-of-mouth advertising gets people coming to try you out. The key on your end is to ensure they have a great experience, excellent-quality food, great service, and a clean environment when they come in that door.

BREAK

These rules have served me well in turning obstacles into opportunities. My work on the board of the NBA Retired Players Association, particularly my tenure as chair, was another prominent example of this mindset in action. The barrier for me was that I had never played in the NBA, nor was I anything close to a star in the ABA. The opportunity was to ascend to the level of president and chairman of the board and help lead the retired players, including some of the past Hall of Fame legends of pro basketball.

I will share the backstory of that experience to provide context. In 1997, the ABA held a thirty-year reunion in Indianapolis, Indiana. The idea was to honor the top thirty players in the ABA's history from 1967 to 1976. The merger between the ABA and the NBA happened in 1976. There was an agreement, but the ABA guys who did not transfer to the NBA were left out in the cold.

The NBA leadership at the time did not like the ABA, and only because of "Dr. J."—Julius Erving—did the merger take place to get him into the NBA. By this time in 1976, I was a successful entrepreneur. I opened the first TGI Fridays in 1995, and it performed exceptionally well. As an ABA player, I had played only three years and was not a well-known player across the ABA institutionally. But locally in Kentucky and Indiana, I had a good base of friends I played with. So, I was invited to the reunion.

I got the idea to look into the opportunity of possibly growing our business by putting together a business portfolio to present to Julius for a Dr. J.–themed restaurant at Disney. I invited the sports information director from Kentucky Wesleyan College, Roy Pickerill, to join me at the reunion and meet the guys. Roy accompanied me and took photos of the entire event, from the autograph session to the formal affair that night, where the top thirty guys were recognized and honored.

After signing autographs that morning, I invited all the players to the closest TGI Fridays to buy them lunch. About forty people showed up, and I had the fortune to visit with each one of them. I presented Dr. J. with the portfolio and spoke with him about the restaurant concept. He took the portfolio, and we got together several weeks later for golf and lunch.

Just before the photo session that night, where all the top thirty guys were to be recognized, Dr. J. asked me to become the secretary of the ABA to help keep all the guys together moving forward. I agreed, and because I had so many names and contact information for ABA associates, I then became the keeper of the ABA files.

Later, in 2002, the NBRPA attempted to grow its membership by adding the ABA players who played at least one year in the ABA. They contacted me once they heard of my ABA files and my relationship with the ABA guys, including the top thirty ABA players, not to mention the contacts I'd made at the Philadelphia NBA All-Star Weekend.

I then assisted the leadership of the NBRPA in including the ABA guys for recruiting purposes. They also offered me a position on the membership committee that was focused on the growth of the NBRPA as it was. I accepted, and later asked to get involved with reorganizing some of the NBRPA restructurings. While participating on the committee, I was asked to run for the board of directors, which I also accepted. I was nominated and won a position on the board.

Once on the board, I was chosen to be the treasurer and a member of the executive committee of that board. I was later voted into the president and chairman position of the board of directors. I was a member of the board for five years. While on the board of directors as chairman, we governed the executive director position and all the retired players of the NBA, ABA, and Globetrotters. This included functions like the NBA All-Star Weekend Brunch, summer meetings and social events for the NBRPA, management of the staff and CEO, and meetings and negotiations with the NBA office and leadership, David Stern, and now Adam Silver.

Over the years, I have also served on other boards, including the United Way board of directors, the Polk Community College Foundation Board, the Florida Bar Foundation and the Boys and Girls Club Board, the Truist Bank Board, and the First Union Bank Board, among others. At my alma mater, Kentucky Wesleyan College, I was on the board of trustees for ten years, from 1995 to 2005, and now serve again on the board of trustees emeritus. Then came the Winter Haven Hospital board.

My service on the NBA Retired Players Board and the leadership of other organizations helped raise my national profile as a former professional basketball player who had become an outstanding and successful African American business entrepreneur. The Tinsley Group, Tampa TGIFriday's development ownership was compromised of myself (51 percent) and Clarence Daniels (49 percent). That was my first venture into the Airport business. Serving in those positions further affirmed my perspective that sharing my story is part of my mission. In the following chapter, I will discuss how my role as caregiver to my late daughter Penni inspired my other mission and my resolve to give back.

CHAPTER EIGHT

HEARTBREAK

Two days of my life will be etched in my memory forever.

The first is April 16, 1976, a Good Friday, the day when my daughter was born. I watched almost breathlessly from my wife Seretha's bedside in the hospital room as Penni arrived. She was delivered by cesarean section, and we were not allowed to be present during the surgery. All of us gathered in the waiting room, including Seretha's mother and stepfather, were caught up in a mix of excitement and nervous anticipation. And then suddenly, there the baby was, in all her beauty, screaming her way into the world.

The second memorable day was Saturday, April 4, 2020, when Penni left this earth. I'll never forget the day I sat at her bedside in our home in Winter Haven, Florida, along with Seretha and George II, as she took her final breath.

This chapter is devoted to the arc of my daughter's life framed by those two days—forty-four years, minus twelve days, apart. These pages are also about the journey Penni and I took together during those years; her life story is also a big part of my own. The relationship she and I had showed me that my self-styled way of turning obstacles into opportunities was helpful in personal as well as professional ways.

Penni's last few years—a frantic rush of doctors, diagnoses, hospital visits, and treatments—posed for me some of the most intense emotional challenges I have experienced. At the same time, the situation offered an unusual chance for me to forge a closer relationship with her, and her with me.

From the moment Penni appeared, the bond between us was automatic, natural, and beautiful. Like most first-time fathers, I had dreamed of having a son. But I prepared myself to heap love on my firstborn from day one, regardless of gender. Seretha and I had tried and prayed so hard for a healthy child for four years. We were married in April 1972, and Penni arrived in April 1976.

Even before Penni's birth, I began doting on her. I guess it's a natural obsession a father has for his child, particularly his first. When Seretha was pregnant, we took part in breathing and birthing classes together. Of course, every day leading up to the birth, my mind churned with thoughts about what fathering would be like.

Even from the early hours and days of her life, it was clear that Penni would love me back. When she cried, no one was able to calm her, so that they would hand her to me. She would look at me, and I would stare straight into her incredible brown eyes, and she would stare back. Then I closed my eyes. And Penni would go right to sleep. From then on, I would become the one who could care for her and keep her from crying. The father-daughter bond was so tight that everyone in the family became quickly aware of it. It enraged my mother-in-law as her grandmother, who only wanted to help and be the one who could calm Penni down for us. "You got some kind of spell on that girl," she would say.

My daughter's name was also a symbol of our bond. My wife's idea was to create a name for our daughter after my original surname, Penebaker. Thus, she came up with Penni.

Throughout Penni's childhood, I would take her to the babysitter in the morning, pick her up in the evening, and take her wherever she needed to go. When she started school, Seretha and I ensured that Penni and her brother got all the support they needed. We stayed in contact with their teachers and administrators throughout their schooling. Through it all, I lavished adoration on both George II and Penni. When Penni was several months old, I remember putting a ribbon on her head, taking her down to Sears and Roebuck's, and taking a picture of her because she was so beautiful and had such a loving smile.

Our father-daughter tie and the unique way she and I communicated with our eyes carried on throughout our lives. It became vital when, years later, Penni was stricken with a fatal illness and became unable to speak. I was her principal caregiver, and we would communicate with one another using our eyes.

PENNI'S REMARKABLE LIFE

But before we get to that emotional phase, I want to first share details about her remarkable life. From her years at school throughout college, Penni was a standout in the classroom, particularly in the performance arts. While a student at Denison Middle School in Winter Haven, Florida, she broke the color barrier by becoming the first African American dance team member. She had become used to being the first African American in many endeavors. But she did not like the status, because it often brought undue criticism from associates and friends.

Penni was an outstanding basketball player also, even though she was not very competitive. She was an extremely accomplished synchronized swimmer, too. She played and was a starter on her middle school and high school basketball teams and reluctantly ran cross-country in her sophomore year of high school. But in her junior year she switched to a performing arts school, and began to focus on acting, dance, poetry, modeling, and art. Those avocations laid the path for a career she later pursued in acting and modeling.

Perhaps more important than the extracurricular activities Penni pursued, what stood out most was her magnetic personality. She was the kind of person who never met a stranger. Everyone was her friend. That willingness to engage with people and help them was a trait she inherited from her mother. She often made helping others a priority above pursuing her own goals.

Penni had natural good looks that grew more enhanced and refined as she grew older. She had my height, and from a facial standpoint, she had the great features of her mom. Her outside beauty was equaled in her inside beauty and thoughtfulness for everyone. Competition was not one of her strong qualities. She didn't achieve what I thought were her dreams and goals professionally due to her desire to help everyone else. When she hit a certain point, she would pivot to giving back to those around her rather than allowing herself to be successful. Maybe that *was* her goal in life that she did achieve.

From the beginning, the door was always open for Penni to be involved in our businesses, at whatever level and whichever way she was comfortable. Her interests and strengths were primarily focused on marketing. She had natural customer service and leadership skills. The people part of marketing was a natural for her. When she encountered difficult areas that she did not know, she would adapt and be a quick learner.

When the business held major events, Penni was there, alongside Seretha, George II, and me, rounding out the team. She saw her role in the company more as a supporter than as an active partner. She did not like the day-in-and-day-out pressure of supervising people. Working in the family business was not always easy for her, being the owners' daughter and coping with the pressures that came along with that, particularly from other employees.

And yet, she brought remarkable acumen to the business. She had the ability to jump into any situation and take ownership in resolving the issue where she worked side by side with me. One example was with a TGI Fridays we had acquired in Lakeland, Florida. We were trying to decide what to do with the business from a leadership standpoint. I had decided to let the general manager go. Penni had just flown home for spring break, and she ended up stepping into this administrative position without any real training and ran the entire operation adeptly for a week and a half. That talent for inserting herself in the middle of messy things and making them right quickly was another skill set she got from her mother. And then, when it was fixed, she'd move to something else. After the Lakeland restaurant was stabilized, Penni's work was done, and she flew back to college, never to return to that Fridays.

Another example of her ability to engage quickly was when we opened our second KFC franchise. Penni was just eleven years old. Something happened at the restaurant that caused me to let most of the employees go. Penni and George jumped in to help. Penni ran the front register, I managed the drive-through, George Jr. worked in the back with the cooks, and Seretha ran the office. With that family teamwork, we kept the business going for a week until we could bring other employees aboard.

I always knew that if I needed her to be there, she would take charge and do what had to be done. But I also understood that being in the family business wasn't her comfort zone. It didn't bother me that much. All I wanted her to do was be successful in her career and put all her energies into that. However, I did want her to continue to play basketball on her high school teams. She would have been very successful, but she had other plans.

Acting and modeling inspired her, and after graduation from the University of North Carolina at Chapel Hill, that was the life she wanted to pursue. New York was the logical place for her to move for this dream. Once she got established there, she spent around 50 percent of her time modeling and acting, mostly in TV roles, and the other 50 percent helping others and trying to find or stay in a job. She was devoted to her friends, a group of nine girls we called The Divas who had been together for years and spent countless times helping in their careers.

On the side, Penni worked in restaurants as a maître d' or server. Every time she would get into a new restaurant, it came out that she had managerial skills and came from a family of restaurant owners. Inevitably, the owners or managers wanted her to be in charge and become a manager. She would do it for a bit but didn't want to get caught up in it. She would say, "I can't do this anymore due to my career," and would move on to another part-time server job.

At times, dating posed complexities for Penni. By the time Penni was in high school, she'd started getting the attention of potential suitors. A cook in one of our restaurants, a likable young man, came to me and said, "Mr. Tinsley, I want to marry your daughter."

I responded, "Then you better get your act together." Penni overheard the exchange. She felt uncomfortable about working among guys who were always staring at her and making comments about her beauty. She didn't like the social pressures that came with the job. She didn't complain, but it was clear that was not what she wanted to do for a career.

One issue that added to her romantic challenges was comparing whoever she may have been dating to me. She also knew that from early high school, whenever guys were interested and wanted to date her, I always wanted to meet and get to know them. Admittedly, I was tough on them. I'd go to the schools, check on them, and do a kind of background check. She appreciated what I was doing, but it still made her uncomfortable.

I recall only two young men coming to the house to visit her. One was during her junior high school years, and the other around graduation. The second one is who took her to the prom, along with her best friend. I drove and chaperoned them to the prom and hung out with them. These kinds of scenarios didn't make dating any easier for her.

PENNI'S ILLNESS

Penni's illness came on without much warning in her early thirties and was a severe jolt to the whole family. Gradually over the years, she lost mobility and the ability to function normally. She relocated from New York to the family home in Florida and was there for the last five years of her life. For the last three she was bedridden.

Throughout that time, I was her primary caregiver. I devoted much of that period to her and working with the home healthcare nurses and doctors. We went back and forth around the state and the South in search of some answers as to what was wrong. For the longest time, it was not clear what the diagnosis was.

The years involved one episode after another of her mom and I scrambling to find a cure and praying for a miracle. In one case, we spent about three months traveling weekly for treatment at the Mayo Clinic hospital in Jacksonville, Florida. We would go up on Sunday evening from Winter Haven and get a hotel room near the hospital. Penni would then go through treatment each day. Then we'd leave Friday evening to return home, turn around, and go right back up the following Sunday.

The years I devoted to caregiving for my daughter changed my overall life and business routines. I still had to keep an eye on the business. The telephone and my laptop became essential tools. Ultimately, I had to delegate many responsibilities in the business to my son, who was primarily working and focusing on our businesses in Miami. I was able to keep a hand in when situations arose that required it. The restaurants that I monitored regularly were within hours of reach by car. It was feasible for me to get in, check on things, make eye contact with the employees, interact with management, and then get back to check in on Penni on the same day. Before Penni's illness, I could travel wherever the business needed me to be.

The caregiving experience also impacted my thoughts about balancing work priorities against those of family. Like many business executives, especially those who obtain success, we had opportunities to grow as big as we wanted to grow, given the available resources. For fifteen years, those opportunities had been coming at a pretty aggressive rate and we were able to take advantage of many of those opportunities. With the caregiving responsibilities, we had to turn a lot down. Being there for the family became more essential.

There was no question that Penni would be my priority. I looked after her, took her to medical appointments, and spent time in the places where she was getting treatment. I needed to work with the doctors, rehab specialists, and home care nurses. And so we readjusted the leadership of the business, having George Jr. take on more responsibilities. My wife ran the office, focusing on the administrative end of the business. With the teamwork we had between the three of us, we didn't miss a beat.

Still, those were not heavy growth years for the business. Thankfully, the infrastructure we built was strong enough to help us through that period, and we remained devoted to Penni through it all. Each member of the family handled her illness differently. It was very tough on George II. There was some natural emotional brother/sister energy going on between him and Penni. It was vital for him to engage with her as often as he could be there.

Once, Penni was reacting negatively to one of her medications. She was jumping around in the bed and talking out of her mind while seeing things. We were concerned, of course, and even contemplated whether we would have to tie her down one evening just to get some sleep.

George II, who was still living in Miami, volunteered to come to stay with Penni through the night. He was in her room at her bedside. He stayed the night until she was relaxed the next morning. He returned to Miami that day, and we wouldn't see him for a while as he recovered emotionally from the experience. But he never stopped communicating with Penni through FaceTime.

Seretha would check in on Penni regularly each morning and evening. The time the two of them spent together was an intensive, quality mother-daughter experience. Seretha knew I would be there for our daughter and stay on top of things, giving her peace of mind.

We also had Sarah, a young nurse's aide who fell in love with Penni from day one and took care of her just like she was her sister. Sarah was with us the whole three years Penni was bedridden, and she became a part of the family. We trusted her to take Penni shopping, to take her to meals, and to doctor visits in her wheelchair. I would often meet them at the doctor's office and sometimes while they were shopping.

By the last four years of Penni's life, we were able to get a diagnosis for her illness: multiple system atrophy. It's a Parkinson's-like rare neurodegenerative disorder. During the last two years, she couldn't carry on a conversation very well. Consequently, we engaged in a lot of one-way communication with hand touching and feeling. When she was a newborn, my daughter and I could speak to each other through eye contact. Just by following her glimpses, I could tell where she was, what her needs were, and if something specifically was bothering her, and I could communicate with her through blinking or body movement.

As we went through all this, I had a lot of time to watch Penni experience this physical challenge and try to come to terms with what was happening to her. The COVID-19 pandemic started to rage just as Penni's health waned. For a couple of weeks after the pandemic hit, we could not see her in person in the hospital. Sarah was able to drive to Tampa from Winter Haven five days a week to be with Penni, given her professional qualifications and licenses, but we were only allowed to visit her by videoconferencing. Of course, we missed touching her and being up close. She wanted to come home.

During that period, we decided to bring Penni home with full awareness that she would not make it. We brought in hospice to take care of her and make her comfortable through her last days. My wife, son, and I spent quality time with her. We also contacted some of her dearest friends to let them know Penni's time was short. On Monday, March 31, 2020, an ambulance pulled into our front drive, and the aides brought my daughter into the house. Seretha, George, and I greeted her.

Her face beamed with joy, and her smile was one I will never forget. It could have lighted up the whole world. For the following days, we relished our time with her. She would squeeze my hand a bit when I spoke to her or asked her a question, but mostly, the communication was with our eyes. I would ask her a question with my voice and my eyes, and she'd blink in response.

Within five days of her homecoming, Penni was gone. Naturally, our family and Penni's close circle of friends fell into a state of sadness. But the lessons of the last few years Penni and I spent together will always stay with me.

LESSONS I LEARNED

As I helped Penni cope with her illness, I gained a new understanding of caregiving for loved ones. My role as caregiver gave me a clarity I did not have before about those who are dedicated and those who were just going through the process. It also let me know, no matter how bad things are in life, it could be worse. The way she was able to handle her personal pain and suffering without complaining one bit and caring for everyone else was amazing. The friends that she had accumulated through her years all came from afar to visit her when they could on the weekends.

When you're undergoing tough times, that's when your true friends are there. Understanding that allowed me to commit more to those close to us as a family. It also renewed my energy to serve the folks in the communities where we do business.

The celebration of life we held for Penni a year after her passing also gave me profound insight. Around three hundred guests came to our house in Winter Haven to remember Penni, all she was, and all she had done. Seeing the family and most of her friends there reminded me of the many lives that she had touched, including those of The Divas, her lifelong friends, her mother, and her brother. But it was clear that there was no life she had impacted more than mine.

Finally, losing my daughter when she was at an early age gave me a different sense of the importance of legacy. In 1972, I found my biological family—my mother and her children, my sisters and brothers on my mother's side, and my father and a sister and brothers on his side. Of these siblings, I have one brother who shares the same mother and father as me. Finding them was critical in building out my sense of family. I had the family that had raised me since being taken in by Mama and my sister Mary and her children. In all, there were sixteen siblings, and I grew to love them all.

The passing of Penni added significantly to my appreciation of family. That deep thinking is what inspired me to write this book. I needed to document my legacy and my family to put it all in perspective.

CHAPTER NINE

IT AIN'T OVER YET

In September 2023, I was invited to speak to students at Florida Southern College's Barney Barnett School of Business & Free Enterprise about my life and career. I shared scenes from my upbringing and career journey, emphasizing events I hoped might resonate with and perhaps even inspire the audience. As I talked, those in attendance, composed chiefly of FSC student-athletes, warmed quickly.

I always gauge the level of interest in an audience by their questions, and this crowd did not disappoint. One student asked how I had dealt with failures. Another questioned how I handled situations I was in when I was judged because of my race. I fielded their queries one by one, trying as best I could to provide mentorship messages that would help these bright young minds positively navigate their college and careers.

Throughout the presentation, I felt wholly in my element. Looking across the audience, I saw versions of myself from decades earlier. I understood the students' state of mind. Just as I had done, they were juggling the twin pursuits of sports and academics, wondering what the most prudent steps to take were as they completed college and entered the world.

As I talked, it was clear that making speeches and giving presentations to audiences is a calling I have cottoned on to. I would even call it a new career direction I plan to follow. The experiences I have already had as a speaker, appearing on stages, in podcasts, and in other public-facing venues, give me pause to reflect on the transformation I have taken from a reserved kid in Louisville who avoided the spotlight to a featured guest on stages speaking to big crowds.

My well-honed way of facing and dealing with obstacles along the way has given me self-confidence. The initial phase of the transformation in my life from a shy kid to a confident young adult started in college. There, when I became more confident in my abilities in sports and the classroom, I was more comfortable garnering the attention of crowds. Where I was once resigned to staying in the background, I now feel at home speaking to big groups.

That comfort, and my biggest motivation to engage in public speaking, stems from an understanding that my lessons could be valuable to others of younger generations who are charting courses like those I have forged. I am mindful that the achievements I have accomplished in business and the status I have been lucky enough to obtain in business and life put me in the fortunate position to give back.

Using part of what I have gained to help others has always been a fundamental aspect of my philosophy, and is at least partly related to my teachers, bosses, coaches, and mentors who have helped me along the way. They inspire me to do for others what they did for me. It's why I became a coach—I wanted to help other athletes just as I had been helped. My upbringing in the church also reinforces my intention to give back. Now that I have a solid record of positive experiences, sharing what I have learned seems to be an appropriate way to give back. Offering talks about the various phases of my life and engaging with audiences is the best way I can think of to follow through on that.

The speech to FSC students was by no means my first or biggest public presentation. I have already had the pleasure of being invited to speak on a wide range of occasions, including giving speeches to colleges, athletes, and business executives. One appearance that stays in my mind was on the stage at Kentucky Wesleyan College, my alma mater, at an event called Pillars, in which the school invites distinguished alums back to speak to students.

Being back on campus brought back a flood of memories, none more vivid than the games I played on the basketball court there. In my remarks, I described many of the moments you've read about in this book from those years of my life. I'd like to think I have a lot to share that is engaging. Over the course of several decades, my life has involved me in many fascinating scenarios. My journeys through school, sports teams, and entrepreneurship often gave way to interesting sagas.

Several of the experiences I typically share never fail to absorb audiences, from my story of working closely with Colonel Sanders to my first KFC burning down, to when my sixth-grade teacher told me just to quit school and go to work, to finding my birth mother and father and the rest of the family. Of course, many other aspects of my life attract interest, too. But I know when I talk about these subjects, many ears will perk up in the audience.

"Everything I learned about myself started when I picked up a basketball and became involved in athletics," I told the crowd. I went on to say:

That was something that I was able to pull from. You don't know what it means regarding confidence in yourself until you have to challenge yourself against another great player. And you go in, whether you win or lose, you come out of it with essential lessons. I learned more from losses than I did from wins. With wins, you tend to celebrate and beat yourself on the chest.

With losses, you step back because it is humiliating. You wonder, why did I lose? Don't blame it on somebody else. Perhaps it's better to ask, how can I improve this team? What can I do to make a positive contribution to this team? In my day, the coach tends to get upfront and show how to do different drills. I paid attention because I was dedicated to doing things the right way. And it paid off. I couldn't throw it in the ocean when I was a freshman. But by the time I was a junior, I was smoking.

Speaking directly to the student-athletes, I said, "Have faith and confidence in what you do, and you'll be successful in this team." I added, "You're going to be successful if you work together and stick together based on what I've seen so far. Follow the lead. Believe in what it's all about. Give it your best effort. You walk off that court if you're tired and don't feel you have anything left. Leave it there, then go back again the next day. I was once a player with the reputation of someone who couldn't shoot. And I went on to help bring about three NCAA D-II national championships and a third place over four years! So, let's get that level of play going back and get the fans back involved. We have had a tremendous fan base here."

I then offered encouragement to the broader audience. "I would say to you, each of you, that you'll encounter things that will get you down. You're going to have to deal with that to feel like it's not working. You've got just to take a step back, suck it up, and go back at it again. Don't let anything keep you from reaching your goal. If you have to go around over the top or straight through, let's just make it happen."

Then came the questions.

"How does it feel to be the first man of color to pledge and join a fraternity on campus?" came one.

"Well, I have tremendous feelings about fraternities," I responded. "Fraternities provide, from my perspective, great camaraderie. But the basketball team has its fraternity as well. It's an individual thing. It certainly can't hurt to join one. But the dedication to education is what you need to do as far as your program is concerned. Think of that first and then consider if you want to get involved in a social organization.

"My fraternity membership opened the door to becoming the king of the campus. I wouldn't have gotten that if I had not been part of the fraternal activities. I had great relationships with my fraternity brothers. We still maintain good relationships today. My dream would be to see Black fraternities and sororities come to this campus, too. It would be fabulous to make that happen. Because that's what this world's all about: diversity, equity, and inclusion."

Another student asked, "Could you give the team one bit of advice that will help us win national championships?"

"Teamwork," I responded. "Working hard, leaving it on the floor, taking on challenges, listening to your coach, even though you're going to disagree with him sometimes and be upset with him sometimes, but he means the best for you and the team as a whole.

"And when you're successful," I added, "reach back and pull others along with you. Reach back. Don't forget where you're going. But you want to give back, and you want to help others be successful as well."

My message of turning obstacles into opportunities and my way of telling stories seems to resonate most with audiences of school kids and students, corporate executives, and athletes. I am comfortable speaking in almost any group of any size, and as I pursue plans to keep engaging in public presentations, I envision speaking to a wide range of audiences. The basketball community, centering around the ABA and NBA alums, has shown a lot of interest in my career, and I can picture making appearances with them. But beyond stage presentations, such as the one I gave at KWC, I have also been a guest on several podcasts, including *Word with Pastor Webb*.

The host, Reverend Reginal T. Webb of Bethel Progressive Missionary Baptist Church in Florida, was exceptionally skilled at raising on-point questions. His questions covered the gamut, with the most significant focus on entrepreneurship and business ownership and what advice I would give others. I used the occasion to summarize my business career, starting with KFC until my leadership at Tinsley Family Concessions.

Franchise ownership was a thrill, I explained. "But I firmly believe that to become a winner, you have to lose," I added. The third KFC we opened and the TGI Fridays in Lakeland were both failed ventures, but as always, I took those obstacles and turned them into opportunities. The TGI Fridays we opened at the Tampa International Airport would become the top-grossing franchise in the chain for nine years running. At its peak, the restaurant brought in $9 million in revenues.

The advice I gave to any budding business executives was this:

- Once you plan that business is something you want to pursue, move quickly to pave your path.

- Seek out mentors, particularly those who are in a similar area of business that you're interested in.

- Be a good listener. When someone with knowledge in business gives advice, soak it up.

- Make an investment of time and energy in whatever area of business your interest lies.

- Get a good education. Whatever area of business you pursue, get a good grounding in accounting—knowing how to balance books matters.

I loved my experience on Pastor Webb's podcast, because he understood and asked what role the church had played in my life. Having been a churchgoer throughout my life, since my childhood in Louisville, I told him, "I would not have been able to achieve what I have without God." I continued, "God has blessed me, and my religion is very much a part of my life and my family's life."

It was a powerful conversation. And in remembering all my past speeches, presentations, panel discussions, and interviews, one thing I realize is that every audience and appearance calls for a different message. This is why I usually prefer to give talks in person, because I like to take time to read the room and provide the audience with a message that will resonate. Students, executives, and athletes are inspired by different stories and in different ways.

When I was called on to give the commencement address at Kentucky Wesleyan College a few years back, this was very much on the forefront of my mind, and I reached inside myself for something that I felt would speak to the diverse crowd.

"Life can be unfair, put blockers in your path, and disappoint you to the point of tears," I told them. "If you maintain an abiding faith, have confidence in yourself, and remain patient, you can and will meet all of life's challenges and find success along the way."

I wondered who heard those words. When a thundering applause came from the audience at the end of my speech, I took it as a sign that the students, teachers, and parents had absorbed my message. That is the real reward to me, seeing the impact sharing my story can have on other people.

Over the years, I have received dozens of awards, plaques, and acknowledgments, and of course, I hold them all close to my heart. Most are displayed on the shelves in my office. But few of those awards have meant more to me than the words of recognition that come with them, and none more so than what the award presenter voiced at the ceremony where I received the Larry Smith Award after being inducted into the Small College Basketball Hall of Fame.

The award, the presenter said, goes annually to a player "who has utilized the game of basketball and its life lessons to promote a better society and promote opportunities for those in need."

I've at this point been inducted into nine different Halls of Fame—the Small College Basketball Hall of Fame, plus the Smoketown Hall of Fame, the Kentucky Wesleyan Alumni Association Hall of Fame, the Black Colleges Athletic Hall of Fame in Kentucky, the Kentucky Athletic Hall of Fame, the Louisville Male High School Hall of Fame (in addition to winning the Louisville Male High Distinguished Alumni Award), the Kentucky Wesleyan College Athletic Hall of Fame, the Softball Hall of Fame in Florida, and most recently the Polk County Sports Hall of Fame—but hearing that specific description of the Larry Smith Award being applied to me filled me with pride and gave me confidence that in following my course of giving back, I was on the right track.

It's a track I plan to remain on as long as I have a voice.

ACKNOWLEDGMENTS

To my wife, Seretha, and brother-in-law, Jerome Hutchinson, who has been a motivating and guiding light as we have developed this book.

To all those who took the time to send testimonials to be included in the book's development. I appreciate each of you.

www.ingramcontent.com/pod-product-compliance
Lightning Source LLC
Chambersburg PA
CBHW020202090426
42734CB00008B/910